D1075047

525

How To Be An Effective Sunday School Teacher

268.007
Ea8h

by
C. B. EAVEY

Price: $1.00

25255

ZONDERVAN PUBLISHING HOUSE
GRAND RAPIDS, MICHIGAN

HOW TO BE AN EFFECTIVE
SUNDAY SCHOOL TEACHER
Copyright 1955 by
Zondervan Publishing House
Grand Rapids, Michigan

Printed in the United States of America

PREFACE

The teaching of a Sunday-school class is one of the few things of importance that people do not hesitate to do without preparation. This little book has several purposes: to awaken prospective and actual Sunday-school teachers to a sense of need for never-ending preparation; to suggest ways in which every Sunday-school teacher should always be preparing; to indicate the necessity for the teacher's considering the pupil and the nature of his learning when he is preparing to teach; to say some things about teaching that he who reads the book may be better prepared for the great work of Sunday-school teaching than he would otherwise be.

Marion Lawrence once said, "Thorough preparation changes drudgery to satisfying pleasure in Sunday-school teaching." The first element of success in anything one does is the determination to succeed. One called to be a Sunday-school teacher can have the satisfaction of success in the measure that he is in fellowship with God through Christ, studies the Bible, has genuine interest in people, and loves the souls of his pupils, if he is inflexibly determined to be always a learner in the inseparable fields of learning and teaching.

It is, however, the miracle, not the method, that makes Sunday-school teaching effective in bringing a soul to life and building it up in Christ. There is, of course, always a means which God uses to bring the soul into full knowledge of the Gospel of Christ. The means, or methods, may vary but the message and the needs of men are unchanging.

CONTENTS

Chapter One

THE TASK OF THE SUNDAY SCHOOL TEACHER

The last command of our Lord was "Go . . . and teach." The teaching task He gave was twofold: to teach so that men might be brought into fellowship with God; to teach those brought into such fellowship the ways of God. From the moment one becomes a follower of Christ, he is not only a learner but also a responsible spokesman for the Gospel of Christ. Each Christian is to teach whenever and wherever he has opportunity. In a general but vital fundamental sense every Christian is called to be a teacher.

The Sunday school is one place where a servant of the Lord can obey the call to teach. It is the privilege and the responsibility of a Sunday-school teacher to be a co-laborer with God in bringing men to Christ, building them up in Christ, and sending them out to bring others to Christ. Essential to effectiveness in Sunday-school teaching is keen realization on the part of the teacher that he is a Christian engaged in work for God. As a worker for God, he will make the most of his opportunities to teach.

The work of God must be done by the power of the Spirit of God. By nature, pupils are dead in sin; their first need is to be made alive in Christ. It is the miracle of God's working, not the teaching, that brings a soul to life. Only the Holy Spirit can draw pupils to the Christ who died that they might have life. Once they are made alive, pupils need teaching so that they may grow in Christ

Jesus. No teacher can grow for a pupil. Each must do his own growing and only the Holy Spirit can guide the soul into that truth which produces growth in spiritual life.

Our Lord, who is called a teacher more frequently than He is called a preacher, said that His Father had "taught" Him. He also said that the Holy Spirit would teach His followers all things. Furthermore, He said, "I can of mine own self do nothing." If our Saviour was utterly dependent on God, how much more so is any human teacher. The Bible record, the history of man, and all human experience unite in testimony to the fact that the teaching of God's Word is effective only when he who teaches it is so completely surrendered to God that the Holy Spirit can work unhindered through him.

This being true, might not a Sunday-school teacher rightly think that there is nothing for him to do? A gardener cannot make a seed or a plant grow. Only God can bring about growth as He does His work through the soil and moisture and sun and rain, in harmony with laws of life and growth that He himself established. Does any gardener conclude, therefore, that there is nothing for him to do? On the contrary, any sensible gardener diligently prepares the soil, carefully sows his seed, and intelligently nourishes growth in terms of the laws and principles that govern it. He knows well that only God can make a seed or a plant grow but he knows fully as well that, for best results, he must cooperate with God while He works.

Likewise, the Sunday-school teacher must work with God but trust Him to do what no man can do. First of all, he must come into, and maintain constantly, right personal relationship with God. Then he must always be learning everything he can about human nature and the pupils he teaches. He must never cease studying the Word of God. He must be a constant student of ways of teaching. He must work diligently before teaching and while teaching each lesson. After he has taught, he must subject results to critical evaluation. No gardener can sit in the chair of do-nothing and have success come to him. Neither can a teacher put forth no effort and be effective.

God never said, "Open your mouth and I will put food in it." Nor does He expect any man or woman to stand before a class, with no preparation either for the work of teaching or for teaching the lesson of the hour, and teach His Word effectively. The kind of teaching He blesses is that done as best the teacher can do it, on the basis of the most thorough preparation he was able to make, while trusting God to work by the Holy Spirit in both him and the pupils. If there were nothing for man to do, our Lord would never have given the twofold command of the Great Commission. The command is to us, not to the Holy Spirit. And the command is accompanied by a promise of the abiding presence of the Lord Himself. When His followers teach, He is with them in the person of the Holy Spirit.

God never changes nor does His message to man ever change. The Spirit-inspired truths of His Word are the same for all men of all time. However, the manner of presenting these truths must be adapted to fit the conditions and the circumstances of those who are taught. There was a time when a good farmer threshed his grain with a flail; the modern farmer harvests with a combine. In an early day, people traveled by ox-cart; today we go by automobile and airplane. He who would be an effective teacher today cannot use the procedures employed by teachers in the days of flails and ox-carts. As is the case in other phases of human activity, so in understanding of human nature, in knowledge of the way in which learning takes place, and in knowledge of teaching procedures, advancement has been made.

Effectiveness in Sunday-school teaching today requires that the teacher take advantage of the best that is available at the present time. Pupils accustomed to modern methods of teaching in the public school are not likely to have much respect for, or to profit from, inferior methods of teaching on Sunday. In the light of the values at stake, the teaching done in the Sunday-school should be better than that done anywhere else. For it to be so, requires, on the part of the teacher, unceasing effort to do the best he can in every situation. The more difficult a situation, the greater is the challenge to effective work.

Any Christian teacher is called to a great task but not to easy work. Recognizing the importance of his calling, the true teacher determines to attain the highest possible proficiency in the performance of his God-given task. He does his best to present himself to God "as one approved, a workman who has no need to be ashamed." With all that he does to prepare himself to be an effective teacher, he never forgets that God's work must be done in God's way, using the means God provides and the method God approves.

Chapter Two

THE TEACHER AND TEACHING

Most Christians, if willing to prepare in all the ways they can, using all the means at their disposal, can become effective Sunday-school teachers. The price of effectiveness is preparation—intelligent, unceasing preparation. It is impossible to drift into any great or high attainment. A lady watching a noted artist draw perfect freehand circles asked him how she could learn to do it.

"You must practice eight hours a day for forty years and then it is just as easy as *this*," said the artist, drawing in illustration a circle as perfect as though made with a compass. It is not easy to state what perfection in teaching is, but well-directed practice leads toward perfection in teaching as it does in anything else.

A person who has never taught can learn how to start in the right way and can then grow in skill and effectiveness while he teaches. One with years of experience in teaching can learn how to become a better teacher. There is no such thing as once-for-all preparation. Effectiveness is dependent upon earnest and continuous study of the work of teaching; preparation is unending. Any Christian can enter upon this study with confidence and assurance, not because he has special gifts but because the Lord who calls His followers to be teachers guides those who obey Him.

The fundamental factor in teaching is the teacher as a person. Teaching is far more than "imparting knowledge," "giving instruction," or "causing another to know." Teaching is the communication of life. The teacher teaches what he is. "The teacher's life is the life of his teaching." The most effective lesson of any teacher is *himself*. No teaching can be better than the person who does the teaching. The better the person, other things being equal, the better the teaching. To be an effective teacher, one must, therefore, ever strive to prepare himself in spiritual life, in character, in social life, in mind, and in body to become continuously a better person.

The spiritual life of the teacher. An effective Sunday-school teacher must be genuinely and thoroughly Christian. Mere profession of Christian faith without possession thereof does not avail. If he does not have the life of Christ in himself, he can hardly teach others the way of life. If he knows the way and will not walk therein, he cannot lead. To teach Christian truth, one must be in the light of Christ and know the inner power of the Spirit of God in his own soul. A teacher cannot very well teach what he accepts with his mind but does not know by way of vital, personal experience.

Sunday-school teaching loses its force when the teacher is not a spiritual Christian. The working of the flesh, though small in amount, kills the spiritual life. Even the constant handling of the Word of God can make him calloused. The teacher teaches what he is at heart. He needs, therefore, constant renewal of spiritual life. He needs to be aware of his carnality and to guard against spiritual loss through unbelief, pride, self-seeking, fleshly indulgence, trifling and sin. Not truly effective will be the teaching of any Sunday-school teacher who condones sin in any of its forms.

To lead his pupils either to Christ or into deeper fellowship with Christ, the teacher must himself be in growing fellowship with God through Christ. Such growth does not just happen. The highest experience known to man—the soul's life in God—must be nourished, and the nourishing calls for man's best powers and his keenest efforts. "Grow in grace and in the knowledge of our Lord and Saviour Jesus Christ" is an admonition to which every Christian teacher who would be effective must give earnest heed. This growth does not occur apart from devotional reading of the Bible, praying without ceasing, constant dying to self, and persistent yielding to God. As surely as the teacher does not keep his heart united to the Lord in humble faith and filled with the presence and the power of Jesus, so surely will it be filled with human folly and vanity. By these his pupils will be influenced, regardless of what he teaches.

An effective Sunday-school teacher maintains a sense of obligation to God. To be prepared to discharge his responsibility to his pupils, he must be keenly aware that he is a servant of God. His is the duty to teach the way of God, and the souls of his pupils are at stake. He has a message needed by them. The emphasis of his teaching is Christ, who came into the world to save them from sin. He is an ambassador of the Lord Jesus Christ. In the measure that he is truly effective, every Christian teacher keeps before himself, first, last and always, the aim of understanding and realizing the tremendous responsibility of his task.

The Sunday-school teacher does not teach merely for the sake of teaching. He does not teach merely that his pupils may come to know the Bible. He does not teach only for the purpose of building up the church. The one definite purpose of the effective teacher is to offer his pupils a living Christ. So long as any pupil is unsaved, the teacher is an evangelist. The knowledge he helps pupils get is, first of all and above all, a means for leading them to accept Christ as Saviour. Once they have done this, he teaches for the purpose of building them up in Christ and for bringing to them the realization that they have responsibility to God for carrying the message of salvation to others.

The teacher with the love of Christ in his heart will see each of his pupils as a soul for whom Christ died. He will teach not that his pupils may know with their minds but that they may have spiritual results in their hearts and lives. Any Sunday-school teacher true to his calling seeks to meet the need of each pupil for salvation or for growth in Christ. Their needs will be varied. Some of any teacher's pupils may never receive any spiritual help except that which he gives them. He may be the only avenue through which these pupils will ever have opportunity to meet God.

A phase of spiritual preparation needed by every Sunday-school teacher is training in the school of prayer. Prevailing prayer is essential in any work done for God. "The Holy Spirit is the means and prayer is the method."

No teacher is fit to teach except as his heart has been prepared by prayer before he meets his pupils. The handling of the Word of God is too sacred a task to be done without prayer. The responsibility of directing souls is too great for a human being to do without dependence on God in prayer. Only as he engages continually and prevailingly in prayer can a teacher be effective.

Likewise, the teacher must prepare himself for constant dependence on the Holy Spirit. Only the indwelling Spirit can make a teacher usable by God. It is God who gives the increase; the teacher is nothing more than a channel through which the Spirit operates in the doing of God's work. The teacher's part is to keep the channel clear by so living, so yielding, and so trusting that the Spirit may work without hindrance to draw the pupils into fellowship with God or into consecration and devotion to God.

The teacher's moral character. The effective teacher must be careful to maintain good works. It will avail little to teach what he does not practice sincerely and consistently. Teaching, however good in content and correct in procedure, cannot take the place of downright, genuine Christian living. One inconsistent act can ruin the effects of months or even years of the best teaching. No teacher can long deceive his pupils. "What you are keeps ringing so loudly in my ears I cannot hear what you say."

There is no substitute for an upright life based upon clearness in thinking about right and wrong and consistency in living according to the highest standards. The standards of the Christian teacher are not the world's standards or the standards of good men and women but the standards set forth by Jesus in His living and teaching. The truly Christian teacher endeavors to live up to these standards. He seeks to be sincere, truthful, honest, just, pure, courageous, strong that he may, in all things, be an example to his pupils. In short, as did Chaucer's parson, he teaches the way of Christ but first he follows it himself.

The teacher as a social being. The teacher who would be effective must be a prepared social person. Man was not made to live alone. Pupils do not learn apart from living. In fact, life is their great teacher. From the day a child is born, he is a member of a group which does things to him and gives him a chance to do things in return. He learns as the forces and persons in his environment act upon him and he reacts to them. As a result of this twofold process, he learns many things, and learns many things well, before a teacher comes into his life. Every person learns far more from living in a social group than he does from being taught formally by a teacher. Whenever he participates actively in living, he learns.

The purpose of Sunday-school teaching is to bring the pupil to Christ and to lead him to love and serve God. How can these ends be accomplished? By having him memorize verses and recite them to a teacher? By requiring him to learn facts and forcing him to drill upon them? By exposing him to a teacher who thinks he is wonderful because he can talk so easily and so much? By so impressing him with the extent of one's knowledge as to cause him to marvel—if he were but given time to think—that "one small head could contain all he knew?" A pupil does not learn to live the Christian life in such ways; if he ever learns to live it, he does so from living with Christians.

Jesus walked and talked with men and women, sharing with them the experience of God. He lived the life of God among the people of His day. He told them in simple, natural, friendly conversation things pertaining to the kingdom of God. The life of God in Him left upon all who came into contact with Him an indelible impression.

And a teacher's vital faith in Christ, expressed naturally in living with pupils as that which he lives by in the depths of his being, makes its impress upon the pupil, awakening him to faith and life.

The individual must do his own learning. He learns well in a situation in which he is living with purposes of his own for engaging in learning, provided he is free to react in his own way and to organize content to fit his purposes. He learns best in a social setting where he and his equals live and learn together under the effective guidance of a teacher who understands them. At its best, teaching is essentially a matter of living with pupils in wholesome, happy, natural fellowship. The teacher is a more experienced person who helps less experienced persons through the sharing of experience and the interpreting of that shared experience.

The Sunday-school teacher has little time for living with his pupils in the school. Over against the thirty minutes—frequently less—that the pupil spends in class on Sunday, he has each week at least one hundred waking hours of time filled with the interests, problems and activities of life. How can the teacher do effective teaching in so small a proportion of time, with so many stronger and more continuous interests and activities taking up the thought of his pupils?

Only by preparing himself in a social way so that he can enter vitally into the whole range of his pupils' living. He must be able to use the few minutes of the class session in relation to the life of the whole week. He must give the session meaning by making it a life situation. Through bringing their interests into the class, he must influence the pupils in the learning they do in living. He must reach out into their living in definite contacts with pupils to share in their total experience. Someone has well said, "A Sunday-school teacher who is only a *Sunday* teacher is not a successful teacher even on Sunday." Learning done apart from living is not lasting, nor are its results usable in life.

To prepare himself for guiding learning through living, the teacher must learn to know people. He must have good understanding of his pupils in general. Then he must understand each of his pupils as an individual. One cannot teach unless he knows and understands the person he teaches. The teacher must also know the people among whom the pupil lives—his relatives and his associates. Moreover, he must be acquainted with the social conditions of the pupil's life and with present-day movements. In short, he must know pupils in their living and the life which they live.

The teacher is a person and the pupil is a person. Real teaching is a series of personal relationships between two persons. To be well-prepared for doing his part in these social relationships, the teacher must cultivate respect for each pupil as a person. The pupil is not an object to be changed. He is not a little being who will some day be a person. Whatever his age, he is a person in his own right. He may be relatively undeveloped and immature but he is a human being with a personality. Any true teacher respects each of his pupils as a person and treats each as a person.

The dynamic for effective teaching is love. Only as the teacher thinks of him as a person and respects him as a person can he truly love a pupil. Any teacher who loves a pupil will find some way to help him. The pupil who knows that he is loved feels secure. Not all pupils are loved by their parents. The love of a teacher may, therefore, give feeling of security never before experienced by the pupil. When he feels secure, his energy is released freely for use in learning activity.

The teacher must also have sympathy—with people in general, with pupils and with each individual pupil. Every person has problems and troubles. No teacher without the sympathetic heart can help pupils as they need to be helped. Harsh, uncritical teaching kills; loving, sympathetic teaching opens the avenues of expression and leads to life. The teacher who respects the pupil as he ought will have the measure of sympathy necessary for teaching him as he ought to be taught.

In his preparation of himself for right relationships with pupils, the teacher should give attention to the cultivation of balance and wholesomeness in his own personality. He must respect his pupils as persons but it is his reponsibility to be, in turn, the kind of person whom they can respect. Since he teaches more by what he is than by what he says and does, he needs to give careful heed to what he is and seek to improve. Anything that makes him a better person will, other things being equal, make him also a better teacher. To teach well, the teacher must be a person who can make all relationships with pupils cordial, sympathetic, interesting, friendly, and free of tension or undue restraint.

For making relationships thus, he should prepare himself along lines such as these: to be cheerful always and to enter actively into the work and the play of pupils; to be consistent, not agreeable and interested one time and impatient and disturbed another time, not lenient at times and severe at other times in respect to the same behavior; to listen sympathetically and with undivided attention to what a pupil wants to say; to cultivate sensitivity for individual differences and to recognize always these differences in dealing with pupils; to let pupils really share in the management of learning activities; to have toward each pupil such an attitude that he will feel free to be himself at all times; to conduct himself so that each pupil can and will act in independence, self-confidence and self-reliance; to have sincere and genuine faith in each pupil.

The intellectual life of the teacher. The teacher's preparation of himself involves his intellectual life as well as his spiritual, moral and social life. In this day, when there are so many educated people in all walks of life, his intellectual development is especially important. A teacher need not be highly educated to be effective but he must learn and grow. Educated or uneducated, the teacher who stops learning ceases to grow. When he ceases to grow, he might just as well stop teaching, for, where there is no growth, there is no usefulness. Pupils will not drink from a stagnant pool and they cannot thrive on a hashed-over diet. The quality of their learning is inevitably determined by the quality of the teaching done by a teacher who should be continually learning.

The Sunday-school teacher who would be effective must forever be growing in his knowledge of the Word of God. This is the content of his teaching. To do good work, he must be thoroughly grounded in it and never cease to study it. He will be a poor teacher if he studies only the lessons he is to teach. No lesson can be taught well except as the teacher is familiar with the entire content of his subject and teaches each lesson in relation to all of that content. The good teacher knows more about a given lesson than he can present in a class session. It matters not that he does not use everything he has, but it is highly important that he have more than he can use. Effective teaching requires not mere mastery of the content to be taught but mastery of content *as it is to be taught.* That is, the teacher must see content from the point of view of his pupils, not merely from his own point of view.

In addition to study of the Bible, the Sunday-school teacher who would teach well will read and study along other lines. Jesus was thoroughly familiar with all the things in His world. Paul at Athens gave evidence of familiarity with Greek poetry. The teacher should seek to grow in all directions. He ought to read good Christian magazines. He needs to be well-acquainted with current events and movements. He should be reading constantly good books in the fields of science, history, poetry, fiction, travel, religion, and such other fields as contribute to healthy development of his intellectual life. Wide reading not only makes him a full man in terms of knowledge useful in teaching, but it also broadens his vocabulary and improves his language and expression. Besides, it gives him a basis for interesting pupils in the development of their minds and for guiding them in their reading.

The real teacher is always a student of human nature. It is forever present with him, waking and sleeping. Besides studying it in himself, he observes and studies it in other people whenever he is in contact with them. Books on psychology, the ways of people and the characteristics of pupils of the age he teaches will be on his reading list. Everything he learns about the ways of human beings is of value in teaching. Constant learning in this field of knowledge keeps him alert to the needs of those he teaches and more capable of directing aright their learning.

Finally, the teacher's intellectual preparation must include study of the theory and practice of teaching. No person can help pupils learn and guide them properly while they learn without considering how to help and guide. An effective teacher must know how to take the learner from where he is to where he should go. To be prepared for doing this, he must at all times be a student of ways of teaching. This is not to say that he must forever be reading books on teaching method. However, it is unreasonable to suppose that any person can do really good work in teaching unless he does do some reading of this kind.

One cannot study profitably the complex activity of teaching except he study it as it is being done by others and by himself. Operating in practice, theory and principles take on meaning. Observation and practice aid the process of absorbing what one reads. The best teaching gives no conscious heed to theory and principles as such, yet it by no means ignores them. He who teaches well does so because he has made a part of himself what he has learned through reading, observation and practice. Constant study is essential for effectiveness in teaching but it produces great results. "Thorough preparation changes drudgery to satisfying pleasure."

The physical fitness of the teacher. An important phase of the effective Sunday-school teacher's preparation as a person has to do with his physical fitness. For zestful action and satisfying outcomes, he needs a body in good condition, one which functions normally in all its parts. A headache, a toothache, indigestion, fatigue or any other untoward physical condition may cause a teacher to say and do things he should not. Absence of malfunctioning makes for clear thinking, concentration of powers and best accomplishment.

It is true that much work for God has been done by people who were not in good physical condition. God does not wait for perfect agents to carry on His work. No one should shrink because he is weak or has minor limitations in body. However, God uses the imperfect physical instrument in spite of its limitations rather than because of them. It is the teacher's duty, as well as his high privilege, to maintain himself at his physical best.

The body is the temple of the Holy Ghost. No Christian, teacher or other, has a right to defile it through misusing it or any of its members. A noted Christian minister once said that he did not believe God would ever forgive the preacher who failed to have his Sunday sermon ready by Saturday noon so that he would have the afternoon free for relaxation and free meditation. If God kept accounts of this kind, what would be recorded against Sunday-school teachers? How many of them teach below the level of effectiveness because they work too hard, keep too late hours, or do something else on Saturday evening that hurts them physically? The wise teacher keeps himself at his physical best for the performance of his great task. He is careful that his body does not come in the way of the working of the Holy Spirit.

Chapter Three

WHAT IS TEACHING?

Essential to effectiveness in teaching is good understanding of what teaching really is. One must think beyond ordinary conceptions to obtain such understanding of the nature of teaching. Most people consider that teaching is telling facts, giving out information, hearing pupils recite, having pupils memorize, asking questions and having pupils answer them, or leading a discussion. True it is, these are some of the many ways of teaching any good teacher may use. It is just as true that a teacher may use any one or all of them and be not merely ineffective but utterly fail to do any real teaching.

A Sunday-school teacher stands before a class of eight pupils and tells them Bible facts for half an hour. One pupil does not understand a single thing the teacher says. Another came to class weighed down with trouble and perplexity about conditions at home and hears nothing because he is preoccupied with these problems. Two pupils spend the half hour in unobserved playing, while two others are conversing and having a good time. None of these four give the teacher the slightest attention. One of the remaining two is much interested in the teacher's manner of talking and gets no connected ideas relating to what is said. The eighth pupil is thinking intently about what he is going to do after the class is dismissed.

Does this teacher teach? If he tells a story which captures the interest of every one of the pupils but has no bearing, in their thinking, on the lesson, will his telling be teaching? If he tells facts so vividly that the pupils listen in spite of themselves yet without interest in what he says, does he teach? If he listens to a recitation that pupils have memorized simply and only because he made an assignment, does he teach them? When he has them repeat verses which they have memorized with no understanding of the meaning thereof, is he teaching? When he leads a discussion on a topic unrelated to the experience of his pupils, does he teach? Does engaging in activity by one called a teacher necessarily mean that he is actually teaching? If answers to questions such as these are negative, what, then, is teaching?

Assuredly, teaching is not engaging in activity for its own sake, however excellent it may seem to be. It is not doing something for the sake of the teacher, however satisfying he may find the doing. When teaching is as it should be, it is primarily concerned with the learner and what is happening to him. It is a matter of working with a pupil in such a way that he learns and grows and becomes what he should be.

Teaching related to learning. Real teaching has to do with a learner in an actual learning situation. There is no teaching without learning and the pupil does the learning. Teaching must take its point of departure from a learning situation and can be understood only in terms of learning. Teaching and learning are two aspects of a single process or activity. Wherever anything is taught, there something is learned not only by the pupil but by the teacher as well. The better the teaching, the better is the learning of both pupil and teacher.

The teacher's part in the twofold activity is to help the pupil learn. An excellent short definition of teaching is: "To teach is to help the pupil to learn." The word "help" implies, among other things, that a pupil learns even when he is not taught. Every normal child learns from the day he is born. Learning is constantly going on from birth until death, or at least so long as the individual has normal use of his powers. Even while he is being taught, any pupil learns many things not taught by the teacher.

All through life the individual learns worthwhile things from the people, the objects, the events and the activities around him, apart from formal teaching. Much of this natural learning is sometimes said to be the result of a process of absorption. However, all learning involves activity; a living being does not take in learning as a sponge absorbs water. Any person, especially a child, does learn many things by copying from others through imitating others and through identifying himself with others. All such learning is done with a minimum of activity on the part of the learner. Secondly, any person, and again the child more particularly, learns much from informal teaching. People round about him—parents, brothers and sisters, others in the home, relatives outside the home, playmates, schoolmates, friends, church associates, tradespeople, fellow workers, business associates, social groups, chance acquaintances, policemen, officials and others—teach effectively many lessons. Thirdly, every person gains much learning from observing objects and people in his world and from experimenting with them.

Natural learning, or learning from living, without the aid of a teacher, tends to be effective learning for these reasons: first, the learner responds to total, meaningful environmental situations; second, he reorganizes his experience as he reacts to these situations, integrating new content with the results of past experience. In formal teaching, the presence and the requirements of a teacher may interfere with the natural manner of response and work against good organization of reactions. Obviously, teaching that is effective must be done according to nature—the nature of the learner and the nature of the learning, two inseparable factors. An understanding of the fundamental characteristics of natural learning is therefore helpful to an understanding of teaching.

Learning, like teaching, is complex and many-sided. No one fully understands the nature of the learning process. In spite of much study by great minds and the formulation of many theories about it, many of its aspects are not clear. However, the more a teacher studies the way in which learning takes place, the better will he understand what must be done in teaching. The better he understands the two, the more effectively can he help pupils to learn.

How learning takes place. The starting point of all learning is a sense of need. A human being is a living, moving, acting being. To be alive implies the necessity of sustaining life. From this main necessity stem numerous specific needs. The presence of need, whether or not it be consciously felt, means a drive or urge to satisfy the need. If it can be satisfied in a routine manner, the drive is reduced and no learning results. If some obstacle or difficulty is met, the individual puts forth effort to deal with a disturbance or upset of equilibrium, and in so doing he learns. Learning, then, is the result of activities engaged in for the sake of satisfying need.

When the individual meets a need that he cannot satisfy in a routine manner, he is confronted with a problem. For example, if he sees something new, he feels a need for knowing what it is. If no answer to the question that arises in his mind comes to him, he has the problem of finding out what the new thing is. This may be a minor problem that he can solve by asking and receiving a satisfying answer to the simple question, What is that? Or it may be a major problem that he can solve only by searching long for a satisfying solution. Whenever a problem is before the mind, the learner has a purpose to solve that problem. Back of this specific and immediate purpose is the remote general purpose to restore his equilibrium which was upset or disturbed when he met the problem. Learning, then, is an outcome of engaging in activity in order to achieve a purpose.

In any learning experience, there are internal conditions—feeling of need, an urge or drive to satisfy the need, and a purpose. There are also external conditions—the objects, persons and events in the environment. The interaction of the two constitute the experience. This interacting begins at birth, if not before. Each learning experience is an essential link in a chain inseparably bound in with all links previously forged. Any particular learning experience is conditioned by the past experience of the learner and by his present environment. When he meets a problem, he begins to study it and to define it in order to see it more clearly. Then he brings up from past experience anything he can that relates to the problem which may suggest solutions. Along with recall of such past experiences, or after their recall, he examines the present environment with a view to finding in it something that may help solve the problem.

From the data thus brought together more or less systematically, he formulates solutions which he tries out in thought. It is probable that he may have to reject his first solutions because he finds them unsuitable. When he finds a solution that seems good, he applies it to the problem to see if it works. If it does not, he repeats the process until he finds another solution to try. As learning progresses, there is a narrowing down toward a point through elimination of unsatisfactory solutions until finally a solution that does satisfy is found.

No normal individual lives his life without facing problems and finding solutions for them. Facing problems is of the nature of life itself. Learning occurs when old ways of acting are incapable of overcoming obstacles to the solution of problems. Environment influences learning. It is from the environment, or at least because of the individual's contact with his environment, that problems arise. The kind of problems met have bearing on both the nature and the quality of the learning. The environment also helps or hinders solution by what it furnishes, or does not furnish, toward solution. Moreover, it gives to learning a certain amount of direction through what it does or does not supply.

The more vital and meaningful the problem an individual faces, the stronger is his drive toward solution. The stronger the drive, the farther does he go in seeking data and the more intense are his activities of searching for, trying out, and judging solutions. In those situations in which he learns best and most, the learner gives himself wholly to the task with consuming interest. With all that is in him, he engages in simultaneous intellectual, emotional and physical activity called forth by his own impelling purpose to solve the problem.

While he is grappling with a problem in the attempt to solve it, the individual looks back at each step and appraises the results of his efforts. Once the problem is solved, he looks back over the completed experience to ascertain how well the purpose of his activity has been realized, wherein it could have been carried on better, and what he can learn from the total experience as a guide to future experience. The essence of all learning is the purpose of the learner that has emerged from activity set in motion by a sense of need which he is trying to satisfy. If the learning is effective, this purpose has been fulfilled satisfactorily in spite of hindrances and difficulties. Learning completes itself in activity engaged in to evaluate the worth of the outcomes of learning—the outcome of each step in the process and the final outcome.

When a person really learns, he grows. The child begins life with initial integration, that is, he functions as a unified whole. Natural learning, if done under wholesome conditions, preserves and promotes integration. Meeting problems, engaging in activity to solve them, recalling and using past experience in new ways, seeing the bearing of present factors, judging the results of activity, trying out solutions, finding suitable solutions, appraising final outcomes—every phase of learning activity brings about growth in personality and life. Things learned while the individual is coping with a problem real to him become part of a meaningful pattern because they are learned in relation to their use. Acquired thus, they promote wholesome development.

Learning under teaching is essentially the same as natural learning. Neither the nature of the person nor the nature of his learning changes just because he is made the subject of formal teaching. It is true that this teaching may hinder him much or help him greatly while he is learning. As was suggested in the preceding chapter, the Sunday-school teacher who would be effective must, in some way or other, enter into the living of his pupils. No teaching has meaning or value to a pupil unless it helps him in his experiences of learning by living.

No pupil ever learns just because he is expected to learn. No pupil ever learns merely because he is in a class. No pupil learns from being sprayed with ideas. No pupil ever learns because of anything said or done by a teacher except as it helps him in connection with the satisfying of needs and the solving of problems. Any pupil learns best when, through his own efforts and for attaining his own purposes, he deals with problems of concern to him—problems he meets in life as he lives it on week-days and on Sunday. It is impossible to separate learning from living. It is just as impossible to be an effective teacher unless one is truly helpful to pupils while they are seeking to satisfy needs and to solve problems actual and real to them.

Need in relation to learning and teaching. The nature of learning, then, determines what teaching is. The starting point of all teaching, as of all learning, is a sense of need—some lack or stress or need of adjusting felt by the pupil, causing him to go into action to deal with a disturbed state of affairs. This disturbance may be minor. Needs may be conscious or unconscious to the pupil; it is not uncommon for a pupil not to appreciate the importance of his need. Whether the disturbance be minor or major, whether or not there be recognition of its existence or appreciation of its importance, the sense of need once aroused continues until the need is satisfied. The initial step in real teaching is to arouse in the pupil the feeling of need. Only as he feels need will he develop purposes and become active in terms of experience meaningful to him. Thus, the teacher may use the pupil's feeling of need for having friends as the basis for teaching him the importance of unselfish behavior.

To bring pupils to awareness of need, the teacher must know their needs. Unless he does, he cannot help pupils become awake to situations they face nor can he guide activities along purposeful lines. Any person's expressed wish, want, or problem may not be at all what he actually needs. A superficial teacher may see as fundamental some external, apparent need when the real need is not evident. All attempts to teach a pupil so long as this actual need is untouched will avail nothing so far as the solution of his problem is concerned. They will tend to deepen need, not to meet it. But the teacher who understands the pupil's needs brings them to the surface of awareness in the pupil's consciousness. Then he guides him into activities acceptable to the pupil in terms of those needs and the purpose he has developed relative to them, thus laying the foundation for effective teaching and learning.

Jesus, by taking the Samaritan woman's need for water as a point of departure, led her to awareness of her need for the water of life. In the case of the young man who asked Him what good thing he might do to have eternal life, He put His finger on his real need of not having his heart set on earthly possessions. The lawyer who sought to justify himself by asking who his neighbor was brought from Jesus the parable of the Good Samaritan which gave him awareness of his need for right attitude toward any one whom he had opportunity to help. A teacher of a class of intermediate pupils realized that they had special need for loyalty to their families. Accordingly, she worked out a unit of five lessons under the title, "Family Life in the Bible." She used the story of Ruth and Naomi to show how happiness can be found through helping one another; the story of David, who was obedient to his father and was used of God; the story of Miriam, who helped her family by taking care of her baby brother; the story of the son of Paul's sister, who warned Paul of danger; and the account of Timothy's grandmother Lois and his mother Eunice, whose faith in God was an example to him. By well-chosen activity in connection with each lesson, she helped her pupils see that people need one another, that each has a part to do in family life, that each should be dependable, and that they should be loyal to those who love them.

Basic needs are common to all people and concern the whole person. Therefore, Sunday-school teaching must make provision for meeting the needs of the whole person. The needs of human beings are so many as to be almost infinite in number. There are basic physical needs such as hunger, thirst, elimination of waste products, sex, temperature maintenance, rest, sleep, the need for escaping pain and discomfort, and the need for physical activity. Other basic needs are the need for mental activity, new experiences, for achieving, to express oneself, for approval, to possess, to compete with others, to develop in one's own way, the need for affection, companionship and sense of belonging, the need to know God, to worship God, and to have fellowship with Him. In addition to basic or primary needs, every child old enough to be taught by a teacher has already developed many secondary needs and drives in the form of desires, likes, attitudes, and—in the case of older pupils—ideals.

To be effective, the Sunday-school teacher must have intelligent understanding and vital appreciation of the needs of his pupils. He discovers and comes to appreciate their needs through his understanding of the Scriptures, his personal experience and observation, his study of human nature, his study of his pupils, and prayer. While his teaching is concerned with the whole person, it is especially interested in the spiritual needs of the pupil. It recognizes as his primary need, right relationship with God through receiving eternal life by faith in Jesus Christ.

Many teachers wonder how they can get and hold the attention of pupils. There can be no effective teaching unless the pupil gives attention to what is being done. The best way to get attention is to capture interest. A feeling of the value, or the worth, of something constitutes interest. No person engages in worthwhile activity except as he sees value in that activity to meet some need. When a pupil does what the teacher wants him to do, without feeling of need, without purpose of his own, without seeing any value in the activity, he is not interested and could not be interested if he tried to be. Let him who would be inclined to doubt this imagine himself doing something that has no point or purpose or value to him and ask himself how deeply interested he would be in that thing.

Effective teaching is a matter of setting the situation so that the pupil feels need, develops purpose to satisfy the need, and sees value in the desired activity to fulfill that purpose and meet that need. His feeling of value spells interest. When he is interested, he will give attention and do all the work necessary for success in learning, provided, of course, that the interest is maintained. And it will be maintained so long as he continues to feel need and has purposes. When a pupil does what he wants to do because he wants to do it, he learns well. The secret of good teaching lies in the ability of the teacher to stimulate desire on the part of the pupil to do the task at hand without any pressure from the outside. A pupil eager to do a thing will bend every effort toward accomplishment and cannot be prevented from learning.

Purpose and teaching. The best teaching, then, utilizes pupil interest based on inner purposes growing out of needs felt. The chosen activity of pupils at any given time is usually concerned with the attaining of purposes which they have adopted. Before they ever come under the care of a teacher, children develop certain general purposes and interests. In helping pupils learn, the wise teacher makes use of the interests pupils already have. He connects these with the work to be done in such a way that more valuable purposes and interests grow out of them.

Teaching is the control of learning so that it will be in harmony with a pre-determined purpose. The teacher must, first of all, have a clear view of the final purpose to be achieved. Then he must select from the vast total of human life those experiences which promote learning and growth toward this ultimate goal. Next, he must arrange these experiences so that this final purpose will be realized. In short, teaching involves control and direction of the environment so that pupils have experiences related definitely to the ultimate purpose of the teaching. This means that the teacher, knowing the needs of the pupils, sets the stage so that from their activity, induced by the presence of felt need, desirable purposes emerge. Pupils will need aid in defining their purposes, in distinguishing between levels and types of purposes, and in choosing those purposes which lead to outcomes in harmony with the ultimate purpose of the teaching.

In addition to the selection and the arrangement of experiences, teaching necessitates stimulating, encouraging and guiding pupils while they learn. The teacher must keep alive the pupil's purpose to solve his problem and thus to satisfy his need. He must encourage the pupil while he is seeking solutions and guide him in developing the implications of possible solutions and in appraising results. In the third place, the teacher must help pupils to manipulate their environment—in their choosing and rejecting of its elements, in exploring the problem and in examining its phases, in adjusting to the environment, and in using it to solve the problem. Finally, teaching must be done with awareness on the part of the teacher that pupils want to learn. Learning is living, and the good teacher does all he can to help pupils in learning and growing and living. This requires alertness to possibilities, ability to take advantage of them, and constant endeavor to help pupils profit well from what they do.

Effectiveness in teaching. Effective teaching is not a matter of native gifts; it does not just happen; it is not automatic; it cannot be done on the inspiration of the moment; it cannot be taken for granted. It involves the setting up of conditions that are best for learning and directing aright the activity of pupils while they learn. It is a matter of organizing and promoting meaningful learning. Always "the teacher should do less teaching and the learner more learning." An effective teacher does not teach —in the ordinary sense of the word. What he does do is to organize the environment and set the stage so that the pupil learns. The important thing in teaching is not the words and the actions of the teacher but what the pupil finds out for himself as a consequence of doing things charged with meaning to him.

The effective teacher does not center attention upon procedures and methods. His question is not, Is this, that or the other method the right one to use? but rather, What influences actually have bearing upon the pupil? His concern is fundamentally with the application in teaching activity, of the principles, laws and conditions of learning. A teacher who has good understanding of these, if he has thorough knowledge of the content he is to teach, can intelligently analyze teaching procedures and learning situations in order to adapt them to what is to be taught. Teaching is not a matter of following rules developed by others. To teach well, one must be able to devise his own procedures for meeting the needs of his particular pupils. It is altogether possible that he can do this better if he has some familiarity with the various techniques of teaching.

This is to say that, whatever the procedure used in teaching, it must have in it something of the teacher himself. It must be something chosen intelligently by him and something to which he makes a contribution of his own. Any teacher can improve in effectiveness by using some new, helpful procedure from time to time. On the other hand, no one need throw away everything he has and start out again with everything new. With even a little background of preparation for teaching, one can be as the well-instructed scribe who, like the householder, "bringeth forth out of his treasure things new and old." But note this: He must have "treasure" from which to "bring forth." It is impossible to get something out of nothing. Effectiveness in teaching is dependent upon the teacher's being a learner while he teaches.

Chapter Four

PURPOSES AND PURPOSING

How shall I begin? is the question before the teacher with a particular class to teach. As is the case with all questions relating to effectiveness in teaching, this one has to be answered in the light of the purpose of the teaching. Without purpose, there is nothing for the teacher to do; learning will go on just as it does naturally, starting with what happens to provide content for experience and going in no certain direction. If the teaching is being done for one purpose, the teacher should begin in one way; if it is being done for another purpose, it may be better to begin some other way. At any rate, both the objectives for the particular lesson and the final purpose of the teaching must be kept clearly in mind from the beginning.

The manner in which he looks upon the class will also have bearing upon the way in which the teacher begins. If he regards the pupils as a group of beings who know nothing and considers himself as a superior all-knowing being who is to dictate what they shall learn, he will begin by telling them what to do. On the other hand, if he thinks of his pupils as a group of persons who are learning and growing together on the basis of what they have already experienced and considers himself also a learner who, because of wider experience and greater maturity, is to direct activities in which all shall share, he begins by presenting objects, situations, problems, or opportunities that awaken purposes.

As was stated earlier, purpose to do something emerges from activity set in motion by feeling of need, whether or not the individual is consciously aware of the existence of the need. The teacher must help pupils to examine and to become acquainted with their needs. The help of the teacher may quicken interests that are felt but not clearly understood. For example, pupils may feel a need for change of position of body and not be aware that this is the cause of their squirming and lack of attention. Or a pupil may have deep need for security and assurance without realizing that this is the basis of his lack of self-confidence. Pupils need assistance also in perception of their needs and interests in relation to like ones of other members of the group. It is essential, too, that the teacher devise ways of relating the purposes of the teaching to individual needs and interests.

An effective Sunday-school teacher is at one and the same time a teacher and a Christian. The purpose of his teaching is, therefore, definitely Christian—to win pupils for Christ and to build them up in Christ. If he is intelligently true to the charge committed to him, his primary concern is with the learning experiences of his pupils as these bring to pass God's purposes in their lives. As Jesus did, the teacher must relate learning to living. Jesus knew the art of teaching. He varied His methods to suit the nature and the needs of those He taught, always basing the method used on some great underlying principle of living and learning.

The good teacher, far from adhering to the use of some technique or device, plans systematically and thoroughly the order of activity of the teaching process. To him, method is a means to an end, an orderly way of proceeding that includes the use of techniques and devices. That with which he is concerned is the applying of sound principles of teaching founded upon the way in which pupils learn. As he works, he develops methods in his approach to teaching problems. Methods flow from situations and personalities. All methods, whatever they are, need to be subjected to examination to be sure that there is nothing in them contrary to principle.

Pupil experience and teaching. Whether a teacher helps or hinders a pupil in learning depends on how he handles him in relation to his experiences. As the pupil responds, so he learns and as he learns, so he *grows and becomes.* This means that teaching, if done effectively, must take note of the on-going experience of the pupil. The activities of learning under such teaching are not evolved out of the opinions and the ideas of the teacher but are vitally related to all the experience—past, present, and future—of the pupil.

The life of any individual is made up of experiences. What any person is, he became through experiences; what he shall be, he will become through experiences. The teacher ought to think less about what a pupil is than about how he came to be what he is and about what he may become through further experience. Every experience an individual has develops him in some way. He is having experience every minute of every day. It takes place through everything he does, simple and complex, guided and unguided, planned and unplanned, satisfying and unsatisfying. From every experience he learns.

Teaching must begin with the experience of the learner, To lead a pupil to where he should go, the teacher must start where the pupil now is. An outstanding characteristic of the teaching of Jesus was His practice of taking something with which His hearers were familiar in experience to bring to them knowledge of the ways of God. In talking to Nicodemus He used the wind as an illustration of the manner of the working of the Spirit in the life of a man. He brought home to the Samaritan woman her need of God by starting with natural thirst, To the crowd on the seashore He taught about different ways of receiving the Word of God by calling attention to the varied results of the sowing of seed. When He wanted to show how men should trust God, He talked of the fowls of the air and the lilies of the field. Over and over, again and again, He *related teaching to the past experience and the present level of development of those taught.* This, every effective teacher must likewise do.

Physical, mental and spiritual experience. Man is body, mind and spirit. More accurately speaking, he is a spirit who has a mind and a body. His experience, therefore, is of three general kinds: physical, mental and spiritual. The purpose of Sunday-school teaching is to bring pupils into a spiritual experience and to cause them to grow in spiritual experience. The Sunday-school teacher is concerned with the physical experiences of hearing and seeing and the mental experiences of perceiving and comprehending only as these are means to the end of his pupils' entering into spiritual experiences. Someone once remarked that a teacher in a secular school would get along much better if pupils came to school without their bodies. In similar vein, it might be observed that a Sunday-school teacher could fulfill better the purpose of his teaching if he did not have to deal with the bodies and the minds of his pupils.

However, there is no way of bringing spiritual truth to human beings as they are here and now except through their bodies and their minds. They cannot believe on Christ unless they have the physical experience of hearing with their ears. They cannot receive Christ as Saviour unless they have the mental experience of perceiving with their minds the facts of the atonement. And they can neither hear nor perceive unless the truth of God is proclaimed. Learning and teaching cannot make pupils children of God; yet, apart from teaching, pupils cannot learn to know God and come into the realization of His purpose for their lives. The conscientious teacher is thoroughly concerned, first of all, with the learning of his pupils because this is the starting point for any experience with God they will ever have.

The laws of learning are the same whether pupils are having experiences in the secular school or in the Sunday-school, whether they are learning history, arithmetic or Bible. The only way pupils can receive content for mental experience is through the senses of the body. The only way the results of physical experience can be made over into mental content is through the operation of the mind. In so far as knowledge for the mind is concerned, teaching is teaching regardless of what is taught. Ways of helping pupils learn in one field or subject, be it English, geography or Bible, are the same as for any other subject —except as the nature of the subject has bearing upon procedure. Bible knowledge is brought to the mind in essentially the same way as any other knowledge is. The Bible, as printed fact, has no magic about it which makes the teaching of its content different from the teaching of any other knowledge for mental experience.

On the other hand, the Bible is the Word of the living God. Under the glorious ministration of the Holy Spirit, when it is heard correctly with the ear and perceived properly by the mind, this Word brings the dead spirits of pupils to life in Christ Jesus and is content for spiritual experience thereafter. The Sunday-school teacher is completely and absolutely dependent upon the Holy Spirit, the third Person of the Godhead, to bring truth to the spirits of pupils. Only God can transmute the content of mental experience into truth for spiritual experience, No teacher can make pupils children of God, no teacher can nurture pupils after they become children of God, except as he works under the power and the influence of the Holy Spirit. Yet to the Sunday-school teacher is committed the charge of so teaching the Bible that pupils will enter into, and grow, in spiritual experience.

A simple illustration may, perhaps, help make clear the interdependence of physical, mental and spiritual experience, and also suggest something concerning the teacher's responsibility. Suppose John 3:16 is being dealt with in a teaching situation. The pupil who merely hears the verse repeated, and gains no understanding at all of its meaning, has physical experience; his only experience is hearing the sounds represented by the words. If, in addition to mere hearing, he gets some understanding of the meaning of the words, he has mental experience also. Now, suppose the pupil thought "Son" was "sun." His physical experience of hearing would be the same, for the two words are identical in sound. But his mental experience would be distorted and would give him no basis whatever for spiritual experience. So long as he thought that the verse told of "sun" instead of "Son," he could not have eternal life.

Experience and effectiveness of teaching. Effectiveness in discharging his responsibility is a matter of the teacher's discovering his part in the pupil's learning experiences and then doing well that part. The pupil must have his own experience; he must do his own learning. All too often in Sunday-schools, the individual who learns most is the teacher because it is he who is most active. No pupil ever learns except as he responds in a properly active manner to influences brought to bear upon him. In other words, *he learns only as he experiences.* Also, *he learns only what he experiences.*

Arranging conditions for purposeful learning. Teaching begins, then, with the arranging of conditions so that pupils have the right kind of experiences. "The right kind of experiences" are experiences motivated by purpose to learn that which is in harmony with the final purpose of the teaching. The arranging of conditions is not done once for all in the beginning; it is a continuous process that has to be carried on throughout the entire course of any teaching-learning activity. Each aspect of learning—purposing, planning, executing and evaluating—consists of many activities and each aspect is present in the learning process from beginning to end. Purposing does have initial importance, but it is not something to be done only in the beginning. Thought division lines cannot be drawn to mark off these phases of learning from one another, each is an experience complete in itself. All may take place at the same time or they may occur in varying order. Each aspect can be shared by pupils in accordance with their individual interests and abilities.

Without a purpose or end that has value for him, a pupil does not learn. The teacher can use primary needs as a basis for interest but these alone do not furnish impelling motives for real learning. Motives have their beginning in the complex acts of living and are the expression of inner purposes that arise from needs felt. "An end which is the child's own carries him on to possess the means of its accomplishment." Any human being has numerous goals or ends—high, low, selfish, unselfish, crude, refined, desirable, undesirable, worthy, temporary, and many others. He is always in motion toward something, even when he does not know what he wants. Every teaching-learning activity should have a clear immediate objective as well as a definite ultimate goal.

For effective teaching, it is essential that pupils share in forming the purposes of their learning activity. It is the teacher's task to stimulate and guide but the purposes should be worked out cooperatively and agreed upon by teacher and pupils together.

Stimulation has for an end the formation of desirable purposes shared by teacher and pupil. The skillful teacher cooperating with pupils does not use compulsion to make them purpose. He assumes the initiative in stimulating but it is the initiative of leadership, not the initiative of force. His leading is done so simply that purposing on the part of the group occurs in the normal course of events, as a wholly natural outcome of the shared activity.

The social setting. This means that the teacher guides so naturally that pupils, unaware of being guided, see and choose purposes in harmony with the final goal of learning. Obviously, this final goal, if perceived at all by pupils, will be clearer to the teacher than it is to them. This kind of guiding requires great skill. It can be done only when the atmosphere of the class situation makes for unrestrained participation. More than any other one thing, the leadership provided by the teacher determines the atmosphere of the classroom. To have a social setting in which pupils will truly cooperate, the teacher must have each pupil feel at ease, have each realize that he has a place in the group, and see that relationships among the members of the group are wholesome.

A primary essential to happy, cooperative relationships in the group is sincere and genuine respect, on the part of the teacher, for each pupil. It is the pupil-teacher relationship that makes for success or failure. The basis for right relationship between the two is the teacher's sincere regard for each pupil as a person in his own right. Along with this, the teacher must have genuine Christian love for pupils. Any teacher who loves pupils gives his attention to them and is absorbed in what serves their best interests. Thoughts of his performance before a group and of his own success do not interfere with his effectiveness in stimulating and guiding. This unreserved giving of self influences and encourages pupils to give themselves in turn.

Then the teacher must be acquainted with each pupil and must help pupils to come to know one another. The teacher who respects and loves pupils with whom he is acquainted is not likely to overwork the perpendicular pronoun. The joy he feels in fellowship with them will prompt, instead, to prevailing use of "we" and "our." This contributes to group consciousness and encourages to active participation. Any true teacher is always a learner with those he teaches. For him, teaching is co-operating with pupils in a friendly, helpful manner while he works hard and eagerly along with them at common tasks.

For a good social setting in which pupils will share actively, it is important also that the teacher treat every pupil with fairness and understanding. Frankness, friendliness, true humility, and work done with no thought of reward or satisfaction for self give the pupils the feeling that the teacher is one of the group. The teacher who best promotes sharing is as ready to accept criticsms of his own acts and ideas from members of the group as he wishes each of them to be. In every way the teacher who leads well shows complete willingness to share fully and unrestrainedly. Thus he helps make an atmosphere for fruitful activity marked by freedom on the part of the pupils.

Beginning where pupils are. To stimulate purposes well, the teacher must begin where the pupils are. He must know their needs, their past experience and their abilities. A pupil cannot develop purpose or interest in anything entirely unrelated to his needs, in anything with which he has had no experience, or in anything for which he has no capacity. No effective teacher is content to understand pupils in general but seeks complete knowledge of the status of development of each pupil. He learns all he can about pupils, observing them as they work and play alone and with others, talking with them, becoming acquainted with their parents, visiting and conferring in their homes, studyng any available records, and talking with former teachers and others who may know the pupils.

To begin where pupils are, the teacher will have to find out what experiences they have had. Purpose emerges from activity engaged in because of feeling of need. However, the nature of any purpose and the direction it takes depend much on the kind of experience the pupils had in the past. For example, the nature and the direction of the purposes developed by a group of pupils from a large city for the study of a unit, "God's Beautiful World," would likely differ from those developed by a group of pupils from the country who studied the same unit. Materials and procedures used successfully in dealing with some pupils at some times may not be effective with other pupils at other times. To stimulate well, the teacher must have understanding of the pupils who are developing purposes at a given time.

The teacher guiding pupils in purposing. Purposing means the choosing, for a particular learning experience, of purposes or goals considered desirable in the light of the ultimate purpose of teaching and learning. In addition to stimulating purposes, the teacher must guide purposing to levels on which the right kind of learning can occur. There can be no learning without purposing, conscious or unconscious, by the learner. For effective teaching, there must be purposing of the right kind. No learning can be better than the purpose for which it is done. The worth of the experiences undergone in any learning situation is largely dependent upon the worthiness of the purpose chosen for engaging in the activity.

The origin of purpose indicates wherein pupils may need guidance in connection with purposing. An individual driven by feeling of need has an impulse to act in some way to satisfy the need. "In some way" implies activity aroused by the drive—activity not consciously directed—just any activity to relieve the tension caused by the existence of the need. As the individual thus engages in impulsive activity, he begins to think. As he thinks, he gets foresight of the possible consequences of acting upon mere impulse. At this point, purpose, or end-view, comes into the picture. It is an outcome of observing conditions and thinking about them and arriving at an understanding of what is involved in the situation and what may result. Along with the choosing of a purpose, the individual begins to plan upon the basis of his foresight of the consequences of acting in a certain way under certain conditions which he understands.

From this, it is evident that pupils may need guidance of several different kinds in formulating purposes. For one thing, they need help in learning to restrain the tendency to act upon impulse. Also, they need to learn not to yield to desire without first observing and thinking seriously about what is best to do. Moreover, it is important that they see clearly the connection between plans of action and the satisfying achieving of purposes. They must learn willingness to pay the price of working persistently at difficult tasks in order to reach a goal determined upon. They must be encouraged to hold to goals, to adhere to purposes once adopted carefully and thoughtfully, until these are achieved. It is altogether possible that plans may have to be modified from time to time but, so long as a purpose once accepted is deemed desirable, there should be no turning from the course leading to its achievement.

The Sunday-school teacher who wants to use the Bible record to help his pupils along these lines has no dearth of material. Moses, smiting the rock, is an example of one who did not restrain the tendency to act upon impulse. Judas betrayed the Lord because he yielded to desire for money without considering the consequences. Eve, likewise, partook of the fruit which appealed to her desire and failed to think of the outcome. Jesus is an example of one who laid plans and achieved purpose. Paul held unswervingly to a goal he had once accepted. Job maintained his purpose to honor God though friends and wife encouraged him to an opposite course of action.

The final duty of the teacher to be mentioned in connection with purposing is to help pupils clarify their intangible goals so that these may serve as real purposes for learning. The purpose of any learning activity must be well-defined in the minds of pupils in order to be of value to them. Unless they have a clear and definite purpose, their learning experience will not be clear and effective. Pupils, especially younger ones, often have difficulty in bringing their vague feelings and concerns into the form of definite personal purposes. Also, they may not know how to express these purposes in words. As the teacher shares in formulating purposes, he can help pupils make their purposes clear-cut and definite. He can also help them to relate accepted purposes to the ultimate purpose of teaching and learning.

All teaching should be done in the light of the present needs and purposes of the pupil taught. There should be no wide gap between the themes of the Bible and the life of the here and now. For example, the teacher of preprimary children should aim constantly to make appeal to their curiosity, imagination, self-interest, affection, imitation and restlessness, using the simple truths of the Word of God adapted to their needs and present interests. The stories of Christ's childhood emphasize the thought of kindness and love, family devotion and unselfishness. His blessing the children suggests His love to them and a sense of intimate relationship. The stories of His kind acts and deeds of helpfulness provide standards of conduct. These Bible stories need to be supplemented with other stories that set forth the qualities and the practices characteristic of the children of God: telling the truth, controlling temper, courage to do good, taking care of themselves, considering the rights of others, being loyal to parents and faithful to home duties. Then the lessons taught may be put into practice immediately in the classroom, in living lovingly, harmoniously, cooperatively and helpfully in relations with others. Thus pupils will be given opportunity for spontaneous reaction to impressions characteristic of children of this age.

Chapter Five

THE PLANNING OF TEACHING AND LEARNING

Once upon a time there was a man who decided to build a house. This man knew scarcely more about a house than that there is such a thing as a house. He had never given a moment's consideration to what is involved in construction activity. He had never troubled himself to observe what a builder does when he builds a house; he knew only that a completed house is composed of stone, brick and lumber. He did not know that there is such a thing as plans or blueprints. This man began to build. He worked diligently for long hours each day over months of time. Naturally, the house he built was a wonder to behold but of little worth as a place to live.

A foolish man, anyone would say. But was he any more foolish than the Sunday-school teacher who engages in activity without purpose, point or plan? Is such a teacher any wiser than a man who builds a house with no thought as to the kind of house he wants and no understanding of what is involved in the building of a house? Will a teacher who works haphazardly get any better results than a man who builds by laying a stone here, sticking in a brick there and nailing a piece of lumber where his unguided fancy indicates?

In temporal matters, men plan painstakingly and laboriously. The architect spends long hours in making careful and detailed plans for even a small building. The engineer works hard over plans for an airplane, a ship, a highway or a new model of an automobile. Manufacturing plants employ at great cost large corps of workers who do nothing but plan. Everywhere in business, industry, commerce and government the necessity and the importance of detailed planning is recognized. How much more necessary is it to develop careful plans for dealing with human beings in respect to spiritual and eternal values.

Obviously, what is not planned is planless and what is planless is likely to be valueless. It is as impossible to teach without planning as it is to rear a great skyscraper or to construct a giant bomber without a plan. If Sunday-school teachers were given to planning their work as painstakingly as builders and engineers plan theirs, Sunday-school teaching would not be on the low level it is. No really good teaching is done by anyone without advance planning. Even after years of teaching experience, any effective teacher keeps on planning carefully and thoroughly. Just as the most experienced engineer or architect must plan each new structure, so the experienced teacher must plan each teaching activity.

The question the intelligent, earnest teacher asks himself continually while he works with pupils is, How can I help *these* pupils to learn? From first to last, his planning is done with the intention to provide the best possible answer to this question. This means that his planning centers upon learning and its organization in the light of the particular pupils, their situation and circumstances, and the conditions and the materials with which he is working. To plan well, he has to use skill in doing three things: selecting and organizing the materials of instruction; adapting these materials and the procedures connected with their use to the needs, interests and abilities of the pupils; and arranging activities so as to bring these materials and procedures into best relation with the pupils' past experience, present purposes and future needs.

Preliminary planning by the teacher. He who really teaches sets the stage for effective learning by careful planning before the pupils come together. He gives attention to the place where the class meets, for physical conditions definitely affect the feelings and the attitudes of pupils. Heating, lighting and ventilation must be right; cleanliness of walls and floor is essential. An attractive, orderly, comfortable place of meeting contributes much to good learning. Everything in its place and flowers and appealing pictures placed at the right height help make a room attractive.

Other classroom matters attended to by the careful teacher include provision for seating in groups as may be best, tables for the use of small groups, cabinets for collections and for storage of materials, interesting and appropriate posters, displays and bookcases as may be needed. Interest centers, browsing tables, pictures, posters, collections and displays are not merely accessories but essentials to effective learning and teaching. When pupils have a share in making plans for these, they are all the more ready to share also in cooperative learning activities.

A third aspect of physical preparation is planning for suitable instructional materials. The teacher should see that plenty of materials are on hand for use as need may arise. Paper, pencils, crayons, modeling materials, workbooks, maps, magazines, books, Bibles, and other printed matter as well as a variety of visual and auditory materials should be available. Teaching is done in a teaching situation arranged by the teacher to help pupils learn. If the aim is to have them to learn to know God's love and care, he can set the stage for learning by putting pictures on the wall and providing books and magazines which show and tell of God's care. If he wants to develop reverence, he can provide a setting which contributes to a sense of reverence. To create settings encouraging to varied kinds of learning, the wide-awake teacher has on hand the materials necessary to set the stage so as to stimulate and guide pupil activity along any desired line.

A most important phase of advance planning by the

teacher is something that has already been mentioned once or twice: his learning all he can about the needs, abilities and backgrounds of pupils. From every possible source, he should gather all the information he can concerning each individual pupil. He should study any available records and test results, become acquainted with home conditions, listen to accounts of experiences, talk informally with pupils, note their choices of activities, books and friends, observe how individuals act in work and play, and use every possible means for gaining understanding of each pupil. Only as the teacher knows the pupil can he really teach him. All the understanding he is ever able to get will be none too much.

Also, the teacher must think beforehand of ways and means for developing wholesome and helpful relationships among the members of the group. To promote relationships most favorable to learning, he will need to take account of things such as these: attitudes of pupils; extent to which they are mutually helpful to one another; manner in which they respond to suggestions; lacks and needs in their personalities; spirit in which they undertake new tasks; how they relate learning to life in general.

The attitudes of the teacher have much bearing upon the success of teaching. When the teacher has good attitudes, pupils are more eager to learn and more cooperative in the work of learning. Some attitudes which the teacher should plan to cultivate and to maintain sincerely and persistently are: zest for continued learning; sincere belief that pupils want to learn and grow; genuine interest in pupils along with real desire and willingness to be of service to them; readiness to use his time and powers in their behalf without seeking anything for self; interest in pupils' interests because they are really interesting to him; confidence in his ability to teach based upon broad general knowledge and diligent preparation for teaching; confidence in his ability to organize the group and its activities for effective learning; sympathetic sharing of pupils' problems because of real concern; cooperative sharing of pupil activities because they are worthwhile in his own mind; recognizing individual differences among pupils with definite attempt to adapt materials and procedures in accordance with these differences; and sincere desire that each pupil develop all his powers in the best way.

Planning the general framework of the content of teaching. Two forms of advance planning must be done by the effective teacher in connection with the materials, or content, of instruction: planning the general framework of the content to be taught and planning the basic subdivisions of this content. Actually, the content framework in which learning experiences are to take place was set up long before the particular teacher was born. It exists in the form of the record of the results of human experience—knowledge, especially as this is made the content of teaching. The real task of planning is concerned with what pupils must do to learn. The problem of planning to teach is how to use the experience of mankind to arouse in pupils the experiences which bring about learning and growth.

From the total experience of mankind, selection and organization of content must be made so that what is presented to pupils is usable by them in the experiences of life as they live it. To plan rightly, the teacher must consider the nature and the type of learning experiences which pupils should have. Their needs, interests, concerns, present level of development, past experience and destiny should serve as guides in determining content to be taught. Nothing in the subject matter is an end in itself. Subject matter exists in the form of knowledge, not pupils. Teaching is concerned primarily with pupils, their learning and growth, not fundamentally with subject matter. "As for knowledge, it will pass away"; pupils live eternally. Knowledge, in itself, is worthless, whether it take the form of a printed book or the words of a teacher.

In general, subject matter represents the results of the experience of the race. The subject matter of Sunday-school teaching is the Bible, the revelation made by God to man in connection with the experiences of life. The Bible is a record of the results of the spiritual experience of the race—of the experience of men with God. God has made Himself known to men through general and special revelation. Shedd says that revelation in its general sense is any kind of knowledge that has God for its source. He also says that, as the term is commonly used, it refers to revelation in a more restricted sense and signifies the written Word of God.

The Bible, the inspired Word of God, is the essential content through which God reaches into the experience of men with His redemptive power. It is the revelation of His truth which came to men right out of their life experiences. God is continually seeking men through their life experiences. He is a living God. He did not say once all what He had to say, then stop speaking. He spoke to men of old and He speaks to men today. The Son of God said, "The words that I speak unto you, they are spirit, and they are life" (John 6:63). God speaks through His Word, by His Spirit, and men can hear Him speaking to them. The experience of the race out of which God revealed His truth in the Bible answers to the experience of men today and becomes the basis for learning the ways of God, receiving the life of God, and growing in spiritual life. The content of Sunday-school teaching is the Bible. It is taught that God may speak to pupils and that they may enter into fellowship and communion with Him.

The whole Bible is content for Sunday-school teaching but the Bible as a whole is not. That is, for a given group of pupils, selection from the whole Bible must be made to fit the life and experience of these pupils. No one ever learns the Bible completely. Learning it completely would be an experience as many-sided as all the lives of all men in all time. Teaching the Bible is not talking about it, telling pupils to apply its truths, and urging them to read it. Teaching the Bible is planning for pupils and setting the stage so that they have experiences without which there is no real and true learning.

Any teacher deeply interested in his pupils might well desire strongly a short cut for them, that is, have them accept without question values that men have found through experience to be important. By so doing, pupils would not be obliged to go through difficulties met by those who went before. However, there is no short cut to growth and development. They do not take place through the transmission of ready-made answers to questions not faced by the learner himself. There is no substitute for experience. A pupil learns as he experiences. He has experiences as he meets needs, problems and difficulties and forms his own purposes relative to them.

Instead of trying to give the pupil results of experience, or knowledge, which cannot be given, the teacher must organize Bible content in terms of learning and growth. Always, he must begin where the pupil is—with things meaningful to him in terms of his past experience. Through these, initial understandings are developed. Then by the use of problems real to him in his daily life and experience, the process of growth is carried to constantly higher levels. It moves upward in the fashion of an opening spiral which rises in ever-widening curves, all of which are but the extension of a point and each of which has its origin in a lower curve. Real knowledge of God may be present from the beginning, can be added to increasingly, and becomes more effective as growth proceeds from the lowest to the highest levels.

Always, the setting must be one of meaningful and purposeful activity on the part of the pupil.

The pupil is the reason for the teaching. It is he for whom learning experiences are provided. It is for his welfare and development that the teaching is done. To provide an orderly and balanced series of learnings, the teacher must control the large framework of the content taught. However, the effective teacher is concerned more with the meaning of the Bible in the experience of the pupil than he is with the Bible as a fixed body of content. For a given pupil, the content is the total of his experiences that are in any way affected by the teaching. As perfect as the Bible is in content, the pupil learns only as he has experiences through interacting with its content. Planning by the teacher has value only as it leads, through selection and organization of content and choice of suitable activities of learning, to experiences needed by his pupil or pupils.

All advance planning by the teacher is tentative. Its basic task is to ascertain what pupils must do in order to learn. A real teaching plan must provide for pupil activities—pupil observing, pupil thinking, pupil purposing, pupil planning, pupil doing. Complete provision for these cannot be made in advance planning. All teaching-learning activity has its roots in the on-going experiences of the pupils. This means that the content for learning is as broad as the lives of the pupils. The learning of any pupil is forever being affected by many influences other than formal teaching. The capable teacher utilizes experiences from family life, school life, and other phases of living, helping pupils to interpret them and to integrate them with the learning experiences of the classroom.

In planning, then, effectiveness involves making a plan for *these* pupils in *this* class, not for pupils in some class at some place. It involves the selection of content that will meet present needs of given pupils in a present situation. It necessitates that the teacher *keep doing his own thinking.* All his decisions in planning ought to be based on consideration of the level of development, the needs, the interests and the abilities of the pupils he is teaching.

Essentials for good advance planning. One of the first requirements of long-range planning, which has been under discussion up to this point, is to determine the aims and objectives to be achieved. That is, what are the knowledges and understandings, attitudes and appreciations, abilities and skills, individual and group behavior forms which the pupils should have as outcomes of their learning? Once these are settled upon, the activities and the materials that will best arouse experiences for the achievement of these objectives must be selected. The statements about selecting and organizing the content of teaching are made with recognition that there are limitations on the freedom of the teacher to select and organize. In most Sunday schools this content is laid out in a series of lesson helps or quarterlies.

Quarterlies and textbooks are printed for the purpose of helping the teacher. Few teachers have either the ability or the time to do all the studying of the Bible, of pupils and of ways of teaching necessary for preparing a series of lessons. Any good quarterly or textbook furnishes directions and suggestions of more experienced persons for the purpose of helping the teacher in his work. These printed productions should be regarded as *helps,* not as something to be followed rigidly. Few quarterlies or textbooks should or can be followed slavishly. The intelligent teacher examines critically the objectives set forth in the printed helps and analyzes carefully the materials and the activities suggested for attaining these objectives. Then he modifies and supplements and complements objectives, materials and activities to fit the situation, the circumstances and the needs of his pupils.

It is possible for any teacher in any school to plan teaching which meets present life needs of his pupils. Any content to be taught can be covered in more than one way. The Bible is so rich in materials essential to the needs of pupils of any and all ages that any portion may be organized and presented in a helpful manner. No school situation is necessarily a barrier to effective teaching and learning. Whatever the teaching situation, the teacher has a group of living pupils with actual needs. One other thing is fundamentally essential: a teacher alert to and informed about these needs, with a sincere desire to guide and help pupils instead of dominating them and compelling them to perform tasks not related to life as they live it and to need as it is present with them.

Obviously, the better the teacher is prepared to teach, the more effectively can he plan. Initial preparation along four lines will help any teacher do better work than he otherwise could. Continuing preparation along the same lines is necessary for continuing effectiveness in planning and in teaching. These lines are: first, knowledge of the Bible and Biblical materials as a basis for leading pupils in their learning experiences. Second, intimate knowledge of the past experience of pupils, collectively and individually, to help the teacher in guiding the pupil's approach to a situation and his reactions thereto. Third, knowledge of mental proccesses and the way in which learning takes place to enable him to anticipate pupil reactions and to plan wisely to meet and direct them. Fourth, a fundamental understanding of teaching techniques and their implications for learning to enable the teacher to meet the general and the specific needs of a learning situation.

Planning the subdivisions of the content of teaching. The second kind of preliminary planning to be done by the teacher is planning the basic subdivisions of the content of instruction. This involves organizing the total work around focal points of purposeful activity or meaningful experience rather than breaking it down into a series of unrelated lessons. These subdivisions are called units. Examples of units are: "How To Get Along with People," "Family Life in the Bible," "Learning from Jesus," "God's Heroes." This phase of planning includes the giving of consideration to the time allotment for each unit and the making of preliminary plans for the handling of each unit.

The essential idea of unit teaching is to organize learning in the natural way. Anyone's life consists of a series of related yet unified experiences. An experience is largely the outcome of preceding experiences, yet each experience has unity in itself. A unit of work is a body of content, a complete whole in itself, organized around a central core of thought but related to units that have preceded and to those that follow. Teaching by units, then, represents an attempt to organize learning experiences to parallel life as it is lived.

The unit idea is essentially the idea of teaching and learning meaningful wholes of content instead of isolated lessons and detached portions of content. The unit plan of organizing Bible content is being followed in some Sunday-school literature. Whether or not the effective teacher finds it in the quarterly he uses, he does his best to follow the idea because it makes for more effective learning on the part of his pupils.

Pupils should share in planning. Whether the plan of organization of content be unitl or lession, pupils should have a share in planning their learning. Obviously, the extent to which they can share is dependent upon their level of maturity and the amount of experience they have had. In planning as in everything else, the teacher should avoid two extremes: doing too much and doing too little. Teacher guidance and direction are necessary. However, as was suggested in the preceding chapter, this guidance should be indirect, unobtrusive and administered by way of good leadership, not thrust upon the group. As the one who is responsible for the learning of pupils, the teacher must do the planning necessary for giving their learning general direction and for relating it to the purposes of teaching. "The teacher must plan so that pupils may plan." Any planning done by pupils will, for the most part, fall within the framework of the teacher's planning.

Teacher-pupil planning cannot be effective apart from adequate preparation by the teacher. He must lay the groundwork in advance of work done by the pupils. However, the teacher should plan neither units nor lessons in any detailed fashion apart from the pupils and he must never thrust upon them any pre-arranged plan. The teacher who has thoroughly thought through the learning possibilities of the area of content for learning and his own objectives in teaching this material is in position to recognize and to follow leads of pupils while they participate in planning. It is the cooperative planning of pupils and teacher that determines the final outcomes in learning that is well done.

As a social group made up of teacher and pupils works together in a real learning situation, purposing naturally shades off into planning. If the teacher skillfully presents objects, situations or opportunities meaningful to pupils in terms of their capacities, needs and past experience they come face to face with questions, difficulties, problems, obstacles and challenges. From the feeling of need thus aroused, they develop a definite and distinct impelling purpose to satisfy the need. As this purpose becomes clear, purposing changes almost simultaneously and imperceptibly into eager planning as further suggestions are contributed and worked over by the group.

Planning is the process of forming a pattern of action, developing means for carrying out effectively the proposed activities, and settling upon the procedures to be followed. It involves organizing and shaping the work to be done and setting in order the steps necessary to take to achieve the accepted purpose.

For effectiveness in teaching, a plan must develop out of an actual situation. It will be a plan that the best and most experienced teacher of even immature pupils could not have foreseen in detail. In any true learning situation, pupils who have a clear grasp of the purpose to be accomplished often contribute most worthwhile suggestions as to ways and means for realizing this purpose. As all members of the group bring from past experience things bearing upon the present problem and together organize these into a pattern, they develop a plan of action for attaining the goal previously recognized and accepted by all.

It is just as necessary that pupils share in planning as it is that they should share in purposing. Sometimes, sharing in planning is difficult. However, when pupils are properly encouraged and guided by the teacher, they enter wholeheartedly into the formulating of plans and they profit greatly from so doing. The skill they develop through many experiences in planning under guidance will help them to meet life situations which call for cooperative planning and action. The amount of help which the teacher should give depends on the maturity level and the past experience of the pupils.

To help them plan their learning well, the capable teacher seeks to lead pupils in thinking through these phases of planning: stating clearly a problem that has meaning to them because it is related to their own lives; finding out what they already know about the matter at hand, by talking over experiences they have had relating thereto and discussing facts and information gained from these experiences; drawing out their questions, evaluating the importance of each question, restating some questions, eliminating others, and listing finally those the group want answered; organizing these questions in terms of specific problems they wish to solve; setting up objectives in terms of behavior changes, general and specific, toward which to work; devising ways to appraise their progress toward their objectives; discussion of available materials needed for learning and where these can be obtained; consideration of experiences which will help to solve the problem; and deciding upon their ways of working—arrangement of room and materials, organization of the group for work, and setting up a tentative time schedule.

Dependence on God in planning. In all his planning—alone and with pupils—the earnest Sunday-school teacher recognizes his utter dependence on God. Here, as in every phase of teaching, he realizes that the work is God's and that he is a channel through which the Holy Spirit operates to accomplish the purposes of God in the lives of pupils. Accordingly, he prays constantly and earnestly, seeks the guidance of the Holy Spirit at every point, and trusts from beginning to end in the wisdom and the power of God not only to enable him to plan and to guide pupils in planning but also to work in and through them as they plan. No amount of purposing and planning engaged in without prayer and trust in God will avail to make teaching effective in saving pupils and building them up in Christ. On the other hand, careful, intelligent planning by a consecrated Christian teacher will make for a much better presentation of the Word of God as the Holy Spirit operates to bring the truth to the hearts of those taught.

Chapter Six

HELPING PUPILS TO LEARN

The practical question before the teacher who has aroused the purposes of pupils to learn and aided them in formulating a plan for learning is, How can I help them learn as they work out their plan? It is not enough that there be a good plan It is not sufficient that pupils engage in activity. It is not sufficient that they have experiences. Not all experiences are good learning experiences. The quality of the learning depends on the quality of pupil experience and the end toward which that experience is directed.

The pupil must do his own learning. He learns as he experiences, reacts and does. Once his interest has been aroused and his purposes really stimulated, he will engage in numerous activities and put forth much effort to get what he wants. The teacher's work is to watch, to guide, to stimulate, to encourage and to offer help when he deems it is needed. His function includes both speaking and being silent. Good teaching can take place without the teacher's saying a word. His attention should be directed away from his own performance and centered upon the doing of the pupil. A teacher can be effective only if he functions in harmony with the fundamental law of all learning: *the pupil learns by doing and experiencing.* Learning begins when the pupil feels need; it advances when the pupil forms purposes to meet his need; it continues with the pupil's planning of ways to achieve his purpose; it progresses as the pupil executes his plan through experimenting, correcting and revising until the purpose is achieved; it culminates in the pupil's appraising of results. To learn, the pupil must do.

Not all doing is muscular in nature. The pupil *does* just as truly when he feels or thinks as when he performs a motor act. Thinking can be so strenuous an activity as to cause great fatigue. A pupil may learn well through the activity of thinking. Feeling may be so intense an activity as to drain away all one's energy. Even when it is not this intense, much of the pupil's best learning is done through the activity of feeling. The pupil learns through doing, then, when he learns to pronounce a word, or draw a picture, when he learns how to reason or to form a judgment, when he learns to appreciate goodness in people or to love the truth, or when he does anything involving physical, mental or emotional activity.

The teacher stimulating and guiding pupils while they learn. Learning is not always easy nor does it take place as a matter of course. Pupils may not have within themselves the resources to carry it to a successful conclusion. Once formed, purposes need to be kept active. Plans made must be executed, and execution requires continued effort. Pupils may become tired, bored, discouraged, uninterested or take on fears and unhealthy attitudes relative to their work. It is not enough that pupils decide what they want to do; they need to be stimulated to carry out their plan and guided while they are carrying it out. From beginning to end, teaching is a matter of stimulating and guiding pupil activity.

Of all the factors external to themselves that stimulate pupils, none is more potent than the teacher and the quality of the teaching. What the teacher is and what the teacher does releases or inhibits the energy of pupils. A cheerful, happy disposition and a human, friendly, cooperative attitude are stimulative. The teacher who stimulates does not let quarterlies and lesson helps come between him and his pupils. He teaches pupils, not content. He is a genuine friend who maintains a personal relationship with each pupil. In the spirit of this relationship, he seeks unselfishly to help each one. The teacher who really respects his pupils, who has sincere concern for them, who shows kindliness and consideration for them, who is interested in and understands them, and who encourages learning and growth, awakens and keeps alive in pupils the desire to learn.

Thorough preparation, involving the gathering of more material than the teacher can possibly use in the lesson, is essential to the stimulation of pupils. Palmer well says, "Why prepare more matter than can be used? Every successful teacher knows. I cannot teach up to the edge of my knowledge without a fear of falling off. My pupils discover this fear and my words are ineffective. They feel the influence of what I do not say. One cannot precisely explain it; but when I move freely across my subject as if it matters little on what part I rest, they get a sense of assured power which is compulsive and fructifying."

Genuine enthusiasm for learning and teaching serves as a stimulant to pupils. A teacher who finds learning fascinating inspires pupils with his enthusiasm. Likewise, a teacher who has a passion for teaching maintains in pupils an interest in learning. If the teacher has good understanding of the learning process and uses learning outcomes in creative and fruitful ways, pupils are challenged. By using sensibly the inclinations of pupils, by appealing to their natural interests, by showing sincere interest in their attainments, and by calling their attention to needs and values, the teacher can keep their purpose alive and active.

Some things the teacher may do to energize pupils for and to guide them in effective learning are:

1. Make objectives definite. Interest is always interest in something. Without specific objectives, there is little

either for appeal to the interest of pupils or to serve as a basis for their purposive activity.

2. Discover the interests pupils already have. The teacher cannot make the pupil interested; all he can do is to build upon interests that are present. He can determine what these are from reading books on psychology and from actual living with pupils.

3. Provide as much first-hand contact with content as possible. There is no adequate substitute for first-hand learning. When things must be learned from vicarious experience, as is often the case, the teacher should make the learning appealing and accurate.

4. Help pupils to comprehend needs they feel but do not completely understand. Teaching must always be done in the light of real needs, not the wants of pupils.

5. Maintain in the classroom an atmosphere of spontaneity and freedom. Pupils are challenged to alertness when they know that they can follow new leads that come unexpectedly.

6. Provide variety in activities. Change is essential to interest and attention. Through change of pace in activity, provision of varied kinds of materials, and the use of different methods of carrying on the work, variety is possible.

7. Keep things moving fast enough to avoid deadening of interest but not so fast as to leave pupils behind.

8. Confront pupils with problems. Without a problem, there is no interest and no fruitful learning. By question, by suggestion, by arrangement of setting, or in some other manner, keep before pupils a problem they want to solve.

9. Ask questions and have pupils ask questions. Good questions incite and guide thought, help pupils analyze complex situations, and assist pupils in forming ideas and in developing ideas.

10. Adapt procedures to individual differences in ability, past experience and interests.

11. Draw all pupils into participation. What affects himself is interesting to an individual. One takes an interest in things which make him feel significant. Besides, any pupil may make a worthwhile contribution to the activity of the group.

12. Introduce pupil cooperation and interaction in place of teacher-centered activity. Satisfying relationships with other members of the group, including the teacher, impel pupils to work to achieve common goals.

13. See that meanings grow. A pupil cannot continue to be interested if he remains where he begins. As meanings grow along with learning, new interests and new purposes should call forth further effort.

14. Keep pupils informed of progress. Knowledge of success not only encourages but also stimulates to continued purposive activity. Praise and commendation often spur a pupil to more intense effort and to new undertakings.

The teacher helping the individual. It is an individual who does his own learning. Though taught in groups, pupils are persons who learn as individuals. All learning is a private, individual matter. Any true teacher is sincerely and deeply interested in each of his pupils as a person. But each pupil is a person who learns. Teaching is, then, a matter of guiding the experience of a person who is a learner, with a view to having his learning benefit him as a person. It is not going through certain motions, ignoring the powers, the capabilities, the desires, the rights and the freedom of the learner and paying no attention to what is happening to him. Its concern is that he come into the fulfillment of that destiny which the God who created him intended and that he grow and develop in his own way.

Though no one knows just how a person learns, it is known that he must do his own learning. The function of teaching is to help him while he is doing his learning, not to force him into a mold of the teacher's choosing. There are many ways or methods which a teacher may use to help a person learn. Some of the most frequently used ones are conversation, telling or lecturing, memorization, discussion, directing games, story telling, recitation, dramatization, reading, directing study, reporting, drill, questioning, audio and visual aids, excursions, committee work, construction work and experiments. Whatever the way used, it is most effective when the teacher maintains the attitude that he is a helper of an individual person who is learning.

The activities of the effective teacher are not based on his own ideas and interests or governed by the content and the methods of instruction. He puts the individual pupil and his interests at the center, encourages him in self-motivated learning, and helps him with his particular problem. At the same time, he welds all the pupils into a social group of which he is one member so that each works for all and all work for each. As the most mature member of the group, the teacher shares his experiences with the other members. Through cooperative planning and working with pupils, he helps each pupil to do what he can do or needs to do, encourages pupil interest, supplies motivation and stimulates to intensive application. Carried on well, cooperative teacher-pupil activity results in the pupil's exercising initiative, assuming responsibility and engaging in critical thinking while directing his own learning. Thus the teacher is relieved of the need of assigning tasks, dominating the classroom and enforcing discipline, and is left free to use his time and energy in guiding pupils as he lives and works with them.

These higher ways of helping pupils learn do not stress teaching techniques as such. The teacher thinks of a class as an active group of persons and makes it that. Both pupils and teacher are concerned with action. They study for the sake of learning. Instead of emphasizing recitation from memory, the doing of required tasks, and the carrying on of verbalized activities, the teacher uses procedures which give the pupils opportunities to do things for themselves. By engaging in constructive activity, performing of experiments, discussion, committee work, asking and answering questions, reading, handling objective materials, and doing other things for themselves, the pupils solve problems that are real to them. Thus teaching becomes what it always is when at its best—a matter of guiding pupils while they learn through study and action.

Telling by the teacher. Helping pupils to learn involves some telling, asking and showing by the teacher. Telling always has been and will always be a common means of teaching. It may take the form of anything from the making of a short statement to the giving of a long lecture. Not always, though, does learning issue from telling. Except as he reacts to the telling, the pupil cannot learn. It is easy to tell a pupil something. Most teachers talk too much—often so much that pupils are hindered in learning. Telling, if done effectively, helps the pupil to learn but it never, in and of itself, results in learning. The pupil learns from the teacher's talking only if he hears, and understands, and reacts to what is said.

To teach by telling, whether in conversing, in giving directions, or in lecturing, the teacher must use words and sentences comprehensible to the pupil. The more simple his words are and the less involved his sentences are, the better will the pupil understand. The purpose of telling is not to entertain, to convey knowledge or to display what the teacher knows but to make contact with the mind of the pupil and to arouse it to activity. The teacher states a fact, a law or a truth, describes an event or tells a story, explains some principle or quotes a statement, recounts an incident or gives a lecture, sets forth an example or an illustration, to provide the pupil with content for use in thinking.

The teacher who speaks distinctly and clearly, using language understood by the pupil, in terms meaningful to his experience and appealing to his interests, reaches the pupil's mind. If he tells, not to impose facts and his own ideas on the pupil but to supply him with information he needs and to confront him with problems he should face, thereby furnishing him with content that awakens mental activity, he helps the pupil to learn.

While there is no good teaching without good talking, or telling, by the teacher, much said by teachers is vainly spent breath. The pupil learns by observing, thinking, judging and reasoning. The measure of the worth of the teacher's talking is the extent to which it induces these activities in the pupil. "There is no royal road to learning"; what a pupil learns, he must work for. Any kind of telling can be a valuable means for sharing the results of experience. On the other hand, if the teacher's talking deprives the pupil of his right to personal participation in activity, it is a liability to learning. Pupil-doing, not teacher-telling, is the key to learning.

The use of questions. Asking questions is an indispensable way of helping pupils to learn. By its use, the teacher can help pupils do their own observing and thinking provided he learns to use it well. The question is fundamental in learning. Expressed or unexpressed, it is present in the life of any normal person. Without wonder, curiosity and doubt, which are the essence of the question, little learning would be done in life. The question is one of the best means for stimulating as well as for guiding learning. It is a means which Jesus used much. The teacher may well study His use of questions. One who would teach successfully must develop ability to ask good questions in the right way.

The unskillful teacher tends to ask too many questions.

He also is likely to be concerned more with getting from the pupil answers which he himself has in mind than with discovery of what the pupil is thinking and to guide that thinking. In general, questions serve well the purposes of learning when they fulfill two basic functions: reveal effectively to pupil and to teacher what the pupil knows in relation to some proposed undertaking; direct successfully the activities of the pupil along suitable lines and hold him to these lines until he reaches a desired goal.

Obviously, it is not sufficient for a teacher merely to ask questions. No amount of questioning will, in and of itself, help a pupil to learn. When they disturb the mental activity of the pupil, when they center on isolated facts, or when they work against the pupil's assuming responsibility for his own active effort, questions hinder learning. A teacher can no more teach by questioning without planning than he can teach in any other way without planning. Good questioning requires ability to think quickly and easily, to adapt readily to changing conditions, and to state questions clearly. Such ability may be native but it can also be developed through experience. Native or acquired, it cannot be used to advantage without previous preparation for the particular teaching situation.

To be effective, questions must be formulated carefully. If a pupil does not understand a question, he cannot respond to it fruitfully. Some characteristics of a good question are: (1) It should be brief, with no more words used than are needed to express the problem adequately. (2) It should be clear, asking one thing and meaning just what it should. (3) It should be simple and precise, without disgressions and double meanings. (4) It should provoke thought. (5) It should be asked in the words of the teacher, not in those of a quarterly or a lesson help.

Questioning should be a two-way matter. The teacher should encourage questions from pupils. A pupil's question often furthers learning better than a teacher's. In a really healthy learning situation, pupils ask more questions than does the teacher.

Showing the teacher. Good teaching includes showing as well as telling and asking. Things seen are more real than the words of either a book or a teacher. More enters the mind through the eye than through the ear or any other avenue. Appeal to eye and to ear in combination makes for better learning than results from a single appeal. There are many types of objective materials which can be used in teaching. Among those suitable for use in Sunday-school teaching are moving pictures, still pictures, models, maps, displays and exhibits, diagrams, outlines, drawings, dramatizations, pantomimes and the blackboard or whatever the teacher or the pupils put on it.

In using audio-visual aids and concrete materials, the teacher should keep in mind that their real purpose is to "aid." They should be used to supplement, not to supplant other activities in learning. No such aid is a substitute for the teacher or for teaching activity. There is no magic connected with audio-visual learning; it is guided by the principles common to all learning. The measure of the value of any aid is the extent to which it promotes learning by enriching and improving pupil understanding of some object, event or activity. It is important that the pupil understand and accept for himself the purposes of the learning experience. The aid should arouse a feeling of need for learning or should be used in connection with other activity which provides this feeling.

No teacher can take a motion picture or any other objective aid into a classroom and use it effectively in teaching without careful previous preparation. He should always preview a film and familiarize himself beforehand with anything he is going to use in teaching. Also, before the presentation in class, he should have a plan formulated and a study guide prepared so that pupils know just what they are to look for. During a presentation, he should give pupils full opportunity for adequate contact and learning, supplement as may be expedient with pertinent remarks, and help them in every way possible. After the presentation, he should summarize the content presented, explain any errors found in it, make necessary additions, encourage class discussion, and test pupils for quality and accuracy of learning.

An effective session where objective materials are used marks the beginning, not the end, of pupil contact with and interest in the content. Any presentation which has accomplished its purpose is followed by more and better questions from pupils than they asked before they saw the objective things. Also, they will be stimulated to further study and investigation along lines suggested by the presentation. The test of the effectiveness of teaching is the extent to which learning is advanced not only temporarily but permanently.

The social aspects of teacher-learning activity. The individual who does his own learning is a social being. He was not created to live alone but to live in company with others. His social needs are just as basic as any of his other needs. Therefore, his learning becomes more meaningful when he shares cooperatively with other learners in the management of his learning experiences.

Teaching at its best is essentially a matter of living with pupils in wholesome, happy, natural fellowship. Teaching rooted and grounded in the fellowship of living together with pupils is vital and meaningful while teaching without fellowship lacks reality. Learning goes on well as living together in shared activities provides fruitful experience in meeting social needs. The basic social needs are: to be loved and wanted; a sense of belonging to the group; and to be like others in ways meaningful to the group. These needs express themselves in drives or urges to belong, to share and to participate.

Of the many things a teacher may do to set the stage for good social relationships in the classroom, these are some of the most important: maintain with pupils a personal relationship marked by mutual respect, confidence, harmony and understanding; give evidence, in all contacts with pupils, of genuine liking for them; understand the emotional problems of pupils, avoid causing these as far as possible and provide adequate outlets for emotional expression; keep himself in good physical, mental and spiritual health; and maintain a social environment in which pupils are sensitive to social conditions, have a feeling of group unity, and share in responsibility and leadership.

In such an environment, activities are natural. Pupils raise questions, offer suggestions, give information, bring in materials, become acquainted with sources, learn how to use materials to get answers to questions, and develop facility in getting knowledge instead of depending on the teacher for facts. They cooperate in planning and doing, in developing initiative and a sense of responsibility, in learning to manage things for themselves, and in attaining skill in working and living with others. All the while, the teacher is at hand as a trusted friend, a true helper, a competent guide, a wise counselor, a ready listener and a capable mature leader upon whom they feel they can depend. He sets the stage for fruitful learning, then he tells, shows, guides, suggests and explains as pupils have need, always learning along with them.

It is not so much the teaching procedure used as it is the spirit and the attitudes of the teacher that is the source of good cooperative participation of pupils in learning together in a group. However, in all teaching, there has to be a way of doing things. Two ways particularly appropriate for use in helping pupils learn in groups are discussion and committee work.

Discussion The discussion technique can be used with pupils of any level, even very young ones. Properly guided by a well-prepared teacher who is a good leader, discussion encourages pupils to be alert, inquiring and active in thinking about problems interesting to themselves. The value of discussion for acquiring information, marshalling thought, molding opinions and attitudes, establishing beliefs, gaining familiarity with a subject, and developing tolerance and consideration of others is unquestioned. There are different types of discussion: teacher-led, pupil-led, committee, whole group, panel, forum, formal, informal and round-table.

Attainment of the values of discussion is dependent upon order and logical development. No two discussions are ever exactly alike but, in general, these six steps should be taken in order: (1) definition and limitation of the problem so that each pupil understands it fully in common with every other member of the group; (2) analysis of the problem which involves consideration of the need for discussing it, its nature, who is affected, misunderstandings or wrong interpretations, and differences of viewpoint; (3) setting of standards to be met by any solution proposed: (4) seeking out and examining possible solutions and their implications; (5) selecting the solution preferred in the light of the evidence gathered during the preceding stage; (6) deciding how the solution is to be put in effect.

Success in guiding discussion either as leader or as teacher with pupil leadership is basically dependent upon two things: extent of teacher preparation and ability of the teacher to lead. The teacher should thoroughly familiarize himself with the topic for discussion, no matter how rich his general background is. This does not mean that he must know everything or that he alone shall judge the worth of comments made. The best discussions are those in which teacher and pupils are learners together. But to guide well, the teacher must be as familiar with the problem and its issues as he possibly can. Always, whether chairman or not, the teacher is the leader of the whole group.

The ability to participate effectively in a discussion has to be learned. Real group participaton in discussion is not easy or simple. Pupils must be guided and they need time in which to perfect their skill and to grow into responsibilities. Over and over again, the teacher will need to note deficiencies and to guide pupils in ways for improving techniques of discussing. They must be led to appraise their progress, to realize wherein they might have done better, and to develop proficiency in participating successfully in the processes of thinking together with others.

Committee work. A second way of guiding group activity is committee work by pupils. It can be used with all pupils except the youngest. Some advantages of learning by working through committees are: it makes for variety in activities in that it brings the whole class into contact with more materials and a greater number of fields of interest than is the case when all pupils do the same thing; it makes possible the participation of each pupil in many activities; from time to time, the teacher can place a pupil in situations especially adapted to his needs at the moment; it brings each pupil into intimate relationship with a number of members of the class; it gives opportunity for presentation to the entire class of the results of work done in smaller groups, and thus helps to build a feeling of belonging, a sense of worth, and self-confidence in pupils.

The size of a committee should be determined on the basis of the work it is to do. It may consist of a single pupil or of several pupils; seldom, if ever, should it have as many as ten members unless most of its work is to be done through subcommittees. The tasks to be performed will determine the number of committees and their assigned duties. Usually, both of these matters should be decided upon by the group. A committee should exist for a purpose, not just to have a committee. A committee is really a discussion group. The teacher should guide pupils in committee work, seeing to it that every member really puts forth mental effort and that there is full opportunity for free exchange of ideas. The teacher should also see that committee memberships are properly distributed among pupils over a period of time so that each pupil has the variety of experiences he needs for his best development. This includes serving at different times on different committees, with different members of the group, and serving in different capacities on different committees —as chairman and as a mere member.

Helping the pupil integrate his learning to form meaningful patterns. The individual who does his own learning as a social being is one piece, so to speak. His experience from the beginning of life to death has a unified oneness; that is, each separate experience is related to all that preceded and to all that will follow. Any good learning experience so changes the learner as to improve the quality of his later experiences. It is what happens in the experiences of the learner that counts. Teaching that truly helps the pupil facilitates the organization of his experience. Learning is a developmental process, not a process of taking in content. It is a meaningful process; it is a process in which understanding counts for much more than does mere repetition. Relatedness is essential to reconstruction of experience. The effective teacher guides the pupil in bringing together continuously the products of learning to form larger and increasingly meaningful patterns of understanding.

Nearly all teaching procedures have possible value in

stimulating and facilitating pupil ability to organize, to integrate or unify the many things learned. The manner in which a method is used counts for more than the method itself does. No one method can be effective in every situation. Any capable teacher uses many techniques and procedures which, in sum total, are a synthesis of methods, not a narrow, mechanized procedure.

Learning is a complex process and any learning situation is highly complex. Any learning experience combines feeling, thinking and acting. Therefore a teaching procedure that limits the pupil to the experience of memorizing and reproducing facts may prevent him from acquiring many other desirable learnings such as understandings, appreciations, attitudes, ideals and skills. Except as all components are attained, complete learning is not a reality. When a pupil really and truly learns, he undergoes an experience involving his whole being, not his ideational powers only. Methods of teaching must take into account the learning outcomes and the learning activities of pupils in relation thereto. Whatever the method used, the pupil must unify various types of outcomes that he is acquiring simultaneously, even if some of these are being attained incidentally as is usually the case.

For effective learning, an experience must begin with and continue to grow out of need real to the pupil. Except as there is ever-present feeling of need, the pupil lacks motivation without which learning neither begins nor continues after it does begin. Purpose to do emerges from activity set in motion by feeling of need. Goals are set up for realizing purposes. Typically, the learning takes on the character of problem solving, with the pupil meeting difficulties and obstacles while he strives to reach his goal. As the process goes on, the learner continues to do the one thing necessary but also enters into many associated activities that help along the central learning activity and result in numerous and varied products. In the measure that the learning is effective, all these activities and their products are continuously unified into larger, more meaningful, more inclusive patterns representing reconstruction and expansion of past experience. As meanings and understandings develop, the learner comes to a point at which he attains insight; that is, his problem is solved, his purpose achieved, his goal reached.

Teaching is concerned, first of all, with a way of organizing activities that is adapted to the needs and the characteristics of pupils as these become manifest during the process. It must provide the content, activities or experiences which will result in the pupil's acquiring all the outcomes essential to complete, well-rounded development. Then it must arouse the pupil to active response and guide his activity toward right goals, aiding him all the while in the integrated remaking of his experience as he reacts to his problems. At the same time, it must be providing sufficient repetition and drill to make permanent those responses which should be enduring. Finally, it must assist the pupil to transfer the results of learning to wider areas of experience.

The problem-solving method. That method of teaching most likely to call for the continuous utilization of previous learnings and the progressive reorganization of the total experience of the learner is the problem-solving method. Problems are numerous and exist in every area of living. The teacher should cultivate an attitude of willingness on the part of pupils to accept challenges in all fields. Problems should be discovered by pupils, not assigned by the teacher or taken from lesson helps. The teacher can help pupils face a problem by asking questions. The nature and the difficulty of any problem must be suited to the maturity level of the pupils. It should also be in harmony with the chosen objectives of learning and should not destroy the continuity and organization of the course. These are other marks of a good problem: it must be clearly stated; it must be interesting to pupils; and it must stimulate good thinking.

Once chosen, the problem must be clearly defined and carefully stated. Next, information must be gathered from past experience and from research as a basis for the formulation of hypotheses, or possible solutions. Each hypothesis needs to be checked or verified until, finally, one is found that seems to constitute an acceptable solution. This solution is then applied. Pupils need help in applying new principles to specific cases, and in modifying their beliefs and judgments in accordance with new ideas and conclusions reached so as to bring the outcomes of problem learning into effective working relationship with their total experience.

The use of telling or explaining as a means for unifying learning. A second means for making learning meaningful, unified and developmental is telling or explaining by the teacher. By telling pupils things about content and explaining aspects of it which they do not comprehend, it can be brought to life in pupil experience. The teacher should, however, never tell or explain what pupils can obtain, without too much inconvenience, or think through, without too much difficulty, for themselves. Also, he should merely tell some things, develop more difficult matters and explain fully only the most complex matters. Usually, telling or explaining has for a purpose helping the pupil to understand and to learn, not the imparting of information. Understanding is both an essential to learning and an important measure of its quality. Ability to explain things so that pupils understand is, therefore, a mark of a good teacher. Any teacher may well study carefully the techniques of explanation.

Supervised study. A third method of teaching for developmental values is supervised study. Pupils need guidance in study though they differ much in respect to kind and amount of help needed. Any capable teacher is alert to the needs of his pupils and shows them how to locate materials, handle tasks, meet difficulties, attack problems, and use their abilities and powers to good advantage, whether or not he does these things in a formal way. In considerable measure, supervision of study is a matter of helping individual pupils. The primary essential is that the teacher be capable of giving good direction and of judging when and how much direction should be given. Then he needs to observe carefully the methods of study of each pupil.

The place of drill in teaching. Drill is a valuable way of teaching when it is part of a larger pattern appealing to pupil interest, understanding, satisfaction and will to learn. It should functon also as a process of differentiation, integration and emerging precision, not as a process of accumulation. Learning is founded upon repetition but mere practice does not make perfect learning. To learn by repetition, the pupil must feel a need for the learning, have a worth-while purpose for the drill, understand what he repeats, and be able to grasp meanings. No amount of drilling will, of itself, change an ignorant pupil into a learned one. He should know the degree of mastery that is expected, he should find drill enjoyable, and he should practice correctly. The teacher should see that the outcomes of drill are used functionally as soon as possible in order that they may be organized and integrated with the outcomes of other learning.

Review as a method of teaching. The final method of teaching to be mentioned is the review. It is activity involved in reorganization and integration of experience after the first learning has taken place. It is a new view of outcomes in a different setting that results in new understandings and new relationships, making for unification of total experience to date. Properly used, it serves the following purposes: to fix in mind things learned; to help the pupil grasp meaningful relationships among the various elements in a body of content; to make more lasting the results of learning; to provide perspective for interpretation of experience; to show wherein the pupil has not learned and the cause of his not having learned; to reveal the causes of teacher failure; and to create new interest in content learned.

To achieve these purposes, reviews should be selective; they should not include everything that has taken place in previous learning. The important ideas and their subdivisions should be concentrated upon. Reviews should be such as to stimulate pupils to coordinate and relate materials and learnings that were acquired at different times and in different connections. A review will be uninteresting if it is merely a re-hashing of old materials. It is the teacher's duty to use techniques of review which provide interesting experiences challenging to pupils. A stimulating review does not just happen; it necessitates considerable thought and careful planning. It is a difficult procedure of teaching, involving critical evaluation, interpretation and integration——and these are not easy tasks.

Chapter Seven

EVALUATING LEARNING

Learning completes itself in the passing of judgment by the learner upon its results or outcomes. Everything a person does is evaluated, more or less perfectly, both by himself and by others. Evaluation is constantly going on in every teaching-learning situation, as it is everywhere else in life. It is exceedingly important at the very beginning, when the purposes of learning are being formed. It occurs at every point in the learning process. Without it, there would be no basis either for planning or for carrying on learning activities. Neither teacher nor pupils would know the value of what was being done. They would, therefore, be unable to continue their planning and working to carry forward the learning.

After teaching and learning have been completed, evaluation is necessary to ascertain how much and how well pupils have progressed in forming habits, skills, attitudes and ideals and how perfectly the ultimate purpose of the learning has been attained. The results of evaluation are a basis for determining what further learning is needed. They indicate to teacher and to pupils what errors need correction, what procedures should be improved, what insights ought to be developed and wherein better adjustment should be made to needs and abilities. Evaluation is a continuous process of appraisal engaged in for the purpose of providing information which can be used in guiding more effectively each pupil while he is learning and growing.

Because evaluation is inseparably connected with the teaching-learning process, pupils need guidance in the continuous use of evaluation. Unless the pupil is guided, he will judge his learning by standards of his own which may or may not be correct and form judgments that may or may not be accurate. Guided well, he will improve procedures and test choices and thus avoid repetition of mistakes. He needs guidance in evaluation that his learning may be properly summarized, generalized and integrated, that he may examine values often and that he may have accurate understanding and proper balance relative to success and failure. And he needs guidance that he may learn to use properly a process he will be using all his life. Learning is not complete apart from evaluation.

All evaluation proceeds in terms of objectives and criteria, or standards, of achievement. Every normal pupil has goals of his own. These may be suitable for learning purposes or they may be the starting point for the development of goals that are suitable. The principle of self-activity applies to the evaluative process as it does to all other aspects of learning. The pupil learns as he reconstructs his experience through planning, executing and evaluating. Not only must the goals be his own but he must also feel responsibility both for judging his progress toward his goals and for appraising the course of procedure he follows in achieving his progress.

One way the teacher can help pupils evaluate is to lead them in discussing how they feel about what is being done and in appraising their plans and procedures. Asking and keeping before them questions like the following helps to keep them aware of the need for continuous appraisal of their work. (1) Are we doing good work? (2) What procedures were all right? (3) Which ones were not so good? (4) What better ones could we have used? (5) What has hindered us most? (6) Wherein have we failed? (7) Where have we succeeded? (8) Should we change our plans in any way? (9) In what ways could we improve upon what we are doing?

In all proper evaluative activity, the individual and his worth is the primary consideration. Instead of setting artificial and unnatural standards, recognition is taken of what each can do with his particular abilities and powers. Neither absolute perfection nor comparison with other pupils is the standard for attainment. What is important is how well each pupil learns in terms of his own purposes in relation to the ultimate purpose of teaching and learning, how fully his needs have been met, and how much he has grown in relation to his capacity for growth.

Recognition that pupils are different and that various levels of individual achievement have real value, genuine respect for each pupil as a person, the necessity for promoting best development in all pupils, realization that growth is satisfactory in the case of each pupil when he makes reasonable progress according to his particular capabilities, and awareness that, whatever the techniques used, evaluation cannot be done mechanically in a way meaningless to teacher or to pupils—these are what the effective teacher always keeps in mind while he guides pupils in the process of continuous evaluation.

With what has been said about evaluation in general, let the Sunday-school teacher consider more specifically the evaluation of the learning of his pupils. Like all teaching, Sunday-school teaching is done to effect certain changes in the pupil through his learning. Any sensible teacher uses those materials and those methods which he deems suitable for achieving the purposes of his teaching. No such teacher lets his pupils carry on this work, engaging in evaluation by standards of judgment devised by themselves. Instead, he guides them as he lives and works with them in friendly, helpful relationships, to appraise their learning well.

Of course, if teaching is content-centered, evaluation is nothing more than a matter of measuring the amount of Bible or other material the pupil is able to remember and reproduce. However, effective Sunday-school teaching has far more important objectives than mastery of knowledge of content taught. It seeks to develop certain kinds of experiences, attitudes, values, motives, loyalties and forms of behavior and conduct. Evaluation of these is much more complex and comprehensive.

Effective Sunday-school teaching produces these outcomes in the lives of those who are taught:

1. Personal, experiential knowledge of God through faith in Jesus Christ as Saviour, with clear ideas and right attitudes concerning God, Christ, sin, salvation, and the Christian's worship, walk and work.

2. Good acquaintance with the contents of the Bible, not as factual knowledge merely but also as a light and as a guide to practical daily living.

3. Understanding of the meaning of living the Christian life, including the ability to distinguish between right and wrong in the sight of God, between Christian principles and worldly greed, and between Christian love and fleshly desires and attitudes.

4. Comprehension of the meaning of and practice in Christian fellowship with the carrying out of obligations to Christ, to church and to fellow Christians.

5. Realization of the need and the responsibility for witnessing, and actual participation in bringing the message of Christ's redeeming love to all men.

Manifestly, evaluation of Christian learning is not easy. To find out how well a passage has been learned, mere recitation suffices. But how can depth of Christian experience or extent of the use of the Bible in personal living be ascertained? Of course, the final test is life itself. The ultimate test of any teaching is the kind of men and women who go out from its influence. The test of Sunday-school teaching is whether it produces Christian men and women.

However, evaluation neither can nor does wait for performance in life situations. As has already been said, evaluation of some kind is inherent in the process of learning. Moreover, after pupils have grown to manhood and womanhood, it is too late to consider the outcomes of their earlier learning activity. It is, therefore, imperative that the work be tested as it is done from week to week, so that every success may lead to renewed effort in the same direction and that every failure may be repaired as soon as possible. The purpose of evaluation is that both teacher and pupil discover wherein learning may be improved. It helps to orient the pupil in work he does now and gives direction to his present efforts.

For Sunday-school teaching, knowledge ends in Christ. The teacher's purpose is not merely to present the Bible. That is important, but it is far more important that the teacher impart Christ. Pupils who receive Christ need guidance and teaching; the new birth marks the beginning of a new life to be nourished. The life of faith is a system of activities of many types. Each activity involves the whole person of the pupil. Some activities are primarily mental while others are predominantly emotional and still others are essentially volitional. Yet none is wholly mental, emotional or volitional. The whole person thinks and feels and wills as a unit, functioning in an integrated manner. The change wrought through and because of Sunday-school teaching is some change in thought, feeling and will involving the whole person. Teaching that is effective brings about learning that takes the learner steadily away from the flesh and its workings and toward maturity and perfection in the life of the Spirit.

Both pupils and teacher may be helped in the process of evaluating learning through the use of some objective data on the results of learning. It is not sufficient to hope piously, to depend on superficial judgment, to follow bias or preference or to guess at indications of progress and measures of achievement. In Christian teaching, the best produced by the mind of man may well be used. Obviously, there are practical difficulties in the use of tests and measurements in connection with the outcomes of Christian teaching. The complexity of Christian experience and Christian living is so great that tests of Christian atttudes, Christian appreciations and Christian conduct have to be made with full recognition of limiting conditions and on the basis of careful inferences.

Many tools and techniques developed for use in secular teaching can be used to excellent advantage by the Sunday-school teacher. Religious educators have devised a number of means for measuring the results of learning; various ones of these have value for appraising the outcomes of Sunday-school teaching and learning. Available tools and techniques include the questionnaire, the rating scale, Bible knowledge tests, life situation tests, the score card, attitude scales, conduct tests, character growth tests, case studies and autobiographical records.

Whether or not it uses data from objective measurement, evaluation of Sunday-school teaching is concerned with changes in growth of activity along lines such as these: giving supreme loyalty to God; maintaining discipleship with Jesus; sincerity and reverence in worship; using the Bible fruitfully; manifesting interest in the spiritual welfare of others; quickening of conscience against sin and evil; crucifying of the self-life; seeking fellowship with other Christians; deepening of prayer life; practicing of stewardship; cooperating in good will with others; and realizing highest potentialities of one's being.

Chapter Eight

EVALUATING THE TEACHING

No more than learning is teaching complete without evaluation. Any alert and capable teacher continuously appraises both the learning of his pupils and the efficiency of his teaching. Every teaching situation impels him to self-appraisal of some kind. There are two general types of evaluation: the easy, unsystematic type and the definite, systematic type. The more objective, definite and conscious the teacher's continuous process of appraising his teaching is, the better can he see the perfections and the imperfections in his work. The greater also will be his insight into the total effects upon pupil learning and growth, of the procedures, activities and materials he uses in teaching.

It is with pupils, their learning, their growth and their lives that the true teacher is concerned. All his activity —evaluative and other—has for its one end and only goal the promoting of the development of his pupils in accordance with the purpose of the teaching. Any conscientious teacher measures his success, appraises his activity and considers his needs for improvement in the light of that which he deems is best for those whom he teaches. In evaluating his teaching, his fundamental interest is not in the effectiveness of some device, technique or method but in how well he has organized and directed learning to meet the needs of his pupils.

In all his planning, even in that done before he meets his pupils, the effective teacher judges carefully the possible value of each contemplated course of procedure. At each and every stage of the teaching-learning process he weighs, more rather than less consciously, the effects and the outcomes of the activity. Over and over again, at points along the way, he examines results critically to ascertain how much and how well the teaching is helping pupils. After the unit or the course has been completed, he subjects to most thorough appraisal the entire teaching process. He watches over every phase of his work—arranging the classroom, stimulating pupils, directing study, planning and organizing instruction, managing classroom routine, sharing, questioning, discussing, telling, showing, drilling, reviewing, evaluating learning—to determine wherein it could be done with greater benefit to pupils.

Through intelligent and continuous evaluation of his teaching, the teacher is able to see wherein he succeeds and wherein he fails. Thus he can capitalize on the successes and repair or avoid the failures. Through evaluation of his teaching, the teacher advances his own learning and growth as a teacher and as an individual. The self-appraisal is valuable in that it enables the teacher to discover the extent to which his teaching effort has been effective so that he can improve old ways and learn new ways of proceeding with his work. As with the pupil, so in the case of the teacher, evaluation helps to orient him and to give direction to his efforts. Except as evaluation is thorough, a teacher works more or less blindly. In the measure that it is done well, the teacher becomes more effective as a teacher.

No teacher worthy of the name is content with low standards, with guessing at results, with careless and superficial judging on the basis of wishful thinking or with groundless faith that things are turning out all right. On the contrary, the conscientious teacher sets up the soundest criteria of effective teaching he is capable of devising, views his teaching activities and the outcomes as objectively as possible and passes judgment upon their effectiveness in as unbiased a manner as he can.

Basically speaking, the best criteria for measuring the outcomes of teaching are a set of principles of teaching founded upon the way in which pupils actually and profitably learn and grow. Perhaps no two teachers would draw up the same set of principles. It is not essential that they should; it is essential that one's ways of teaching be in harmony with the manner in which pupils really learn. The teacher's evaluation of his teaching becomes, then, a matter of relating his methods, procedures and product to his principles of teaching.

One way of appraising is for the teacher to observe his own teaching as objectively as possible. To stand himself in a corner, as it were, and to look at his teaching as impartially as he would look at the teaching of another teacher can help any teacher see wherein his teaching is good and wherein it lacks. Any teacher can also learn much about the quality of his teaching by bringing it into comparison and contrast with the work of other teachers whom he observes while they are teaching.

To derive the best from observing teaching—his own or another's—a teacher must observe with intelligent discrimination between the essential and the unessential. It is easy to center attention on meaningless details and overlook significant aspects. That which should be noted are the factors which make for good learning or the absence of it. The observer should see how the teacher succeeds and where he succeeds, why he fails and where he fails, in helping pupils to learn. To do this, the observer must concentrate attention upon the behavior of the pupils, not upon the activities of the teacher. How the pupils respond and what they do are far more important than what the teacher does, because their learning is the measure of the success of the teaching. Most necessary is it that the observer not yield to his prejudices. He should make all his judgments, favorable or unfavorable, on the basis of actual conditions, not in the light of his likes and dislikes. Finally, the observer must do some thinking in connection with what he sees. He must ask questions of himself and reflect upon what he sees.

Somewhat more objective than observation is the use of check lists for instructional activity and rating scales of teaching efficiency. The use of such devices from time to time gives any teacher a good basis for appraising the quality of his work. The careful examination of one's work in the light of the content of good articles and books on teaching is a means of evaluation. Attendance at conferences on teaching and talking freely with other teachers can supply a teacher with data for evaluation. The attitudes and the opinions of pupils can be helpful to a teacher in evaluating his teaching. An alert teacher detects many of these subjectively in the normal course of teaching.

Any teacher sincerely desirous of knowing how he is doing might have other teachers observe his teaching at times to appraise it. Likewise, he can profit from the critical reactions of others, such as superintendents and parents of pupils. A truly effective teacher is so absorbed in perfecting his teaching ability that he is willing to learn from appraisal by anyone so long as the judgment expressed affords him some basis for learning how to pass better self-judgment on the quality of his teaching.

The teacher's evaluation of his teaching cannot be considered apart from its product. This is a pupil who has become what the teaching was done to make him be. Sunday-school teaching begins with what man is by nature but it proceeds with the destiny that may be his through grace. The two aspects are implicit in the command Jesus gave His followers. "Go ye therefore and teach" to the end that those taught may become new creatures in the family of the redeemed; "teaching them to observe all things whatsoever I have commanded" to the end that they may grow in the life to which they have been won.

It is the power of God that makes pupils new creatures. No teaching, be it ever so perfect, can make a pupil alive. Life is in Christ. "He that believeth on the Son hath everlasting life: and he that believeth not the Son shall not see life; but the wrath of God abideth on him" (John 3:36). "He that hath the Son hath life; and he that hath not the Son of God hath not life" (I John 5:12). Effective Sunday-school teaching does not "pretend to draw education out of human nature itself and evolve it by its own unaided powers." Christian faith is not something that was discovered by the mind of man and it cannot be entered into through the learning process. It was revealed by God through Christ and is made actual in a pupil's life by the operation of the Holy Spirit. The first step in Sunday-school teaching is so to present Christ as Saviour that he who is taught may, as the Spirit operates, believe and pass from death to life.

Once the pupil is born again, the new life must be nourished that it may grow. Like all life, it must have food. On the quality of the food it receives will depend the direction and the vigor of its growth. To provide the right food in the right amount and in the right way is the task of effective teaching. This teaching must be carried on in complete dependence on the Holy Spirit and in prevailing prayer. Only He who imparts life can nourish that life; through prayer the teacher can lay hold on His help. No more than his Lord who said, "I can of mine own self do nothing," can a Sunday-school teacher do his work effectively without the help of God.

The pupil, a new creature in Christ Jesus, learns and grows that he may become perfect in Christian personality. The goal of all Christian teaching, as expressed in the words of one of its greatest teachers, is to "present every man perfect in Christ Jesus" (Col. 1:28). The standard by which the effectiveness of Sunday-school teaching must be judged is nothing less than the man of God, "perfect, throughly furnished unto all good works" (II Tim. 3:17).

Date Due

OCT 9 '58
OCT 14 '58
OCT 22 '58
OCT 22 '58
NOV 4 '58
NOV 11 '58
JAN 19 '59
APR 13 '59
OCT 6 '59
NOV 28 '59
DEC 8 '59
FEB 8 '60
MAY 23 '60
NOV 28 '60
DEC 12 '60
JAN 4 '62
OCT 22 '62
5/27/63
DEC 17 '63
FEB 7 '64
FEB 21 '64
JAN 4 '65
JAN 23 '65
MAY 5 '65
APR 13 '67
APR 29 '67
MAY 10 '67
10/12/68
MAR 9 '71
NOV 7 '72
OCT 24 '78
DEC 14 1982
MAY 21 1985
OCT 22 1985
MAY 13 1992
OCT 25 '06

PRINTED IN U. S. A.